Contents

About the Authors

MARK DEVER (PhD, Cambridge) is the pastor of Capitol Hill Baptist Church in Washington, D.C. and the president of 9Marks. He is the author of more than a dozen books, including *The Church: The Gospel Made Visible* and *Discipling: How to Help Others Follow Jesus.*

JONATHAN LEEMAN (PhD, Wales) is the editorial director for 9Marks and is an elder at Capitol Hill Baptist Church in Washington, D.C. He is the author of a number of books on the church, including *Don't Fire Your Church Members: The Case for Congregationalism* and *Political Church: The Local Assembly as Embassy of Christ's Rule.* Jonathan also teaches at a number of seminaries.

ROBERT BRUCE JAMIESON III (PhD candidate, Cambridge) is an affiliated lecturer in New Testament Greek at the University of Cambridge. He is a member of Eden Baptist Church in Cambridge, where he lives with his wife and three children. He previously served as an assistant editor for 9Marks, and he is the author of *Going Public: Why Baptism Is Required for Church Membership.*

PHILIP NATION (DMin, Southeastern Baptist Theological Seminary) is a publishing leader, a pastor, and an author. His latest book is *Habits for Our Holiness: How the Spiritual Disciplines Grow Us Up, Draw Us Together, and Send Us Out.* He regularly blogs about faith, life, and leadership at *philipnation.net*. Philip developed the content for week 3.

Portions of this Bible study were adapted from the following books in the 9Marks Church Basics Series (B&H Publishing, 2016).
Understanding the Congregation's Authority by Jonathan Leeman
Understanding Baptism by Jonathan Leeman and Robert Bruce Jamieson III
Understanding the Lord's Supper by Jonathan Leeman
Understanding Church Discipline by Jonathan Leeman
Understanding Church Leadership by Jonathan Leeman and Mark Dever
Understanding the Great Commission and the Church by Jonathan Leeman

DISCIPLE *for* LIFE

Basics

UNDERSTANDING THE FOUNDATIONS
OF A HEALTHY CHURCH

Robert Bruce Jamieson III, *Mark Dever,*
Jonathan Leeman, & Philip Nation

LifeWay Press®
Nashville, Tennessee

Published by LifeWay Press®
© 2016 9Marks, Mark Edward Dever, Jonathan Leeman, and Robert Bruce Jamieson III

ISBN 978-1-4300-5514-3 • Item 006104044

Dewey decimal classification: 262
Subject headings: CHURCH / CHURCH POLITY / DOCTRINAL THEOLOGY

To order additional copies of this resource, write to LifeWay Resources Customer Service; One LifeWay
Plaza; Nashville, TN 37234-0113; fax 615.251.5933; call toll free 800.458.2772; order online at lifeway.com;
email orderentry@lifeway.com; or visit the LifeWay Christian Store serving you.

Printed in the United States of America

Groups Ministry Publishing • LifeWay Resources • One LifeWay Plaza • Nashville, TN 37234-0152

Introduction

Jesus Christ established the church. Rather than have Christians try to grow and accomplish God's mission as individuals, Jesus has called us together to carry out His kingdom work. The Bible describes the church in many ways, such as the bride of Christ, a body, and a family. It's crucial for us to learn how to relate to Jesus as a church body.

*Understanding the foundations of the church
helps us be healthy church members.*

In His Word God has given us the stories of the first-century church, as well as authoritative teachings about what it means to be the church. As we travel through Scripture together, we'll learn and respond to God's call for Christians to work together as the church.

Over the next six weeks we'll look at the foundations of a healthy church:

Congregational authority
Baptism and the Lord's Supper
Stewardship
Church discipline
Church leadership
The Great Commission

Our prayer is that you'll see how wonderful it is to be a part of a healthy church. God has given us a beautiful gift by connecting our lives together. We'll see that the everyday work of the church is something that, when done in relation to one another and in the power of the Holy Spirit, brings about great spiritual maturity and glorifies God.

How to Use This Study

This Bible study book includes six weeks of content. Each week has an introductory page summarizing the focus of the week's study, followed by content designed for groups and individuals.

GROUP SESSIONS

Regardless of the day of the week your group meets, each week of content begins with the group session. This group session is designed to be one hour or more, with approximately 15 to 20 minutes of teaching and 45 minutes of personal interaction. It's even better if your group is able to meet longer than an hour, allowing more time for participants to interact with one another.

Each group session uses the following format to facilitate simple yet meaningful interaction among group members, with God's Word, and with the video teaching by a group of trusted pastors.

Start

This page includes questions to get the conversation started and to introduce the video segment.

Watch

This page includes key points from the video teaching, along with space for taking notes as participants watch the video.

Discuss

These two pages include questions and statements that guide the group to respond to the video teaching and to relevant Bible passages.

Pray

This final page of each group session includes a prompt for a closing time of prayer together and space for recording prayer requests of group members.

INDIVIDUAL DISCOVERY

Each *Disciple for Life* small-group resource provides individuals with optional activities during the week, appealing to different learning styles, schedules, and levels of engagement. These options include a plan for application and accountability, a Scripture-reading plan with journaling prompts, a devotion, and two personal studies.

This Week's Plan

Immediately following the group session's prayer page is a weekly plan offering guidance for everyone to engage with that week's focal point, regardless of a person's maturity level or that week's schedule.

You can choose to take advantage of some or all of the options provided. Those options are divided into three categories.

Read

A daily reading plan is outlined for Scriptures related to the group session. Space for personal notes is also provided. Instructions for using the HEAR journaling method for reading Scripture can be found on pages 8–11.

Reflect

A one-page devotional option is provided each week to help members reflect on a biblical truth related to the group session.

Personal Study

Two personal studies are provided each week to take individuals deeper into Scripture and to supplement the biblical truths introduced in the teaching time. These pages challenge individuals to grow in their understanding of God's Word and to make practical application to their lives.

LEADER GUIDE

Pages 120–31 at the back of this book contain a guide that develops a leader's understanding of the thought process behind questions and suggests ways to engage members at different levels of life-changing discussion.

The HEAR Journaling Method for Reading Scripture

Daily Bible Reading

Disciple for Life small-group Bible studies include a daily reading plan for each week. Making time in a busy schedule to focus on God through His Word is a vital part of the Christian life. If you're unable to do anything else provided in your Bible study book during a certain week, try to spend a few minutes in God's Word. The verse selections will take you deeper into stories and concepts that support the teaching and discussion during that week's group session.

Why Do You Need a Plan?

When you're a new believer or at various other times in your life, you may find yourself in a place where you don't know where to begin reading your Bible or how to personally approach Scripture. You may have tried the open-and-point method when you simply opened your Bible and pointed to a verse, hoping to get something out of the random selection from God's Word. Reading random Scriptures won't provide solid biblical growth any more then eating random food from your pantry will provide solid physical growth.

An effective plan must be well balanced for healthy growth. When it comes to reading the Bible, *well balanced* and *effective* mean reading and applying. A regular habit is great, but simply checking a box off your task list when you've completed your daily reading isn't enough. Knowing more about God is also great, but simply reading for spiritual knowledge still isn't enough. You also want to respond to what you're reading by taking action as you listen to what God is saying. After all, it's God's Word.

To digest more of the Word, *Disciple for Life* small-group Bible studies not only provide a weekly reading plan but also encourage you to use a simplified version of the HEAR journaling method. (If this method advances your personal growth, check out *Foundations: A 260-Day Bible-Reading Plan for Busy Believers* by Robby and Kandi Gallaty.)

Journaling What You HEAR in God's Word

You may or may not choose to keep a separate journal in addition to the space provided in this book. A separate journal would provide extra space as well as the opportunity to continue your journal after this study is completed. The HEAR journaling method promotes reading the Bible with a life-transforming purpose. You'll read in order to understand and respond to God's Word.

The HEAR acronym stands for *highlight, explain, apply,* and *respond.* Each of these four steps creates an atmosphere for hearing God speak. After settling on a reading plan, like the one provided in this book in the section "Read" each week, establish a time for studying God's Word. Then you'll be ready to HEAR from God.

Before You Begin: The Most Important Step

To really HEAR God speak to you through His Word, always begin your time with prayer. Pause and sincerely ask God to speak to you. It's absolutely imperative that you seek God's guidance in order to understand His Word (see 1 Cor. 2:12-14). Every time you open your Bible, pray a simple prayer like the one David prayed: "Open my eyes so that I may contemplate wonderful things from Your instruction" (Ps. 119:18).

H = Highlight

After praying for the Holy Spirit's guidance, open this book to the week's reading plan, open a journal if you'd like more space than this book provides, and open your Bible. For an illustration let's assume you're reading Philippians 4:10-13. Verse 13 may jump out and speak to you as something you want to remember, so you'd simply highlight that verse in your Bible.

If keeping a HEAR journal, on the top line write the Scripture reference and the date and make up a title to summarize the meaning of the passage. Then write the letter H and record the verse that stood out and that you highlighted in your Bible. This practice will make it easy to look back through your journal to find a passage you want to revisit in the future.

E = Explain

After you've highlighted your verse(s), explain what the text means. Most simply, how would you summarize this passage in your own words? By asking some simple questions, with the help of God's Spirit, you can understand the meaning of the passage or verse. (A good study Bible can help answer more in-depth questions as you learn to explain a passage of Scripture.) Here are a few good questions to get you started:

- Why was the verse or passage written?
- To whom was it originally written?
- How does the verse or passage fit with the verses before and after it?
- Why would the Holy Spirit include this passage in the Bible book?
- What does God intend to communicate through the text?

If keeping a HEAR journal, below the H write the letter E and explain the text in your own words. Record any answers to questions that help you understand the passage of Scripture.

A = Apply

At this point you're beginning the process of discovering the specific personal word God has for you from His Word. What's important is that you're engaging with the text and wrestling with the meaning. Application is the heart of the process. Everything you've done so far coalesces under this heading. As you've done before, answer a series of questions to discover the significance of these verses to you personally, questions like:

- How can this verse or passage help me?
- What's God saying to me?
- What would the application of this verse look like in my life?

These questions bridge the gap between the ancient world and your world today. They provide a way for God to speak to you through the specific passage or verse.

If keeping a HEAR journal, write the letter A under the letter E, where you wrote a short summary explaining the text. Challenge yourself to write between two and five sentences about the way the text applies to your life.

R = Respond

Finally, you'll respond to the text. A personal response may take on many forms. You may write an action step to do, describe a change in perspective, or simply respond in prayer to what you've learned. For example, you may ask for help in being bold or generous, you may need to repent of unconfessed sin, or you may need to praise God. Keep in mind that you're responding to what you've just read.

In this book or in your journal, record your personal application of each passage of Scripture. You may want to write a brief explanation-and-application summary: "The verse means _____ , so I can or will _____."

If keeping a HEAR journal, write the letter R, along with the way you'll respond to what you highlighted, explained, and applied.

Notice that all the words in the HEAR method are action words: *highlight, explain, apply, respond.* God doesn't want us to sit back and wait for Him to drop truth into our laps. God wants us to actively pursue Him instead of waiting passively. Jesus said:

> Keep asking, and it will be given to you. Keep searching, and you
> will find. Keep knocking, and the door will be opened to you.
> **Matthew 7:7**

Congregational Authority

The church is amazing. As God assembles Christians together in a group, He allows us to be a blessing to one another, a collective witness to the world, and a means of displaying His glory on the earth. God Himself has ordained that Christians work together in what He's named the church.

As we study the basic nature of the church, we want to start with simply holding the whole idea in wonder. It's amazing that God has saved us and allowed us to be a part of His covenant people.

As we take time to study, discuss, and pray, we should do so with both joy and humility. To the church God has given His great message of redemption. With this message we carry an unexpected authority.

This week we'll seek to understand the congregation's authority. When we hear the word *authority,* it often simply conveys the idea of making decisions. But the Lord has so much more in store for believers in the way we exercise authority. The authority God gives to the church is to carry out a primary command from Jesus: to make disciples (see Matt. 28:19).

To discover how we're to use the authority God has entrusted to the congregation, we need to better understand the makeup of a church and how God instructs us to operate as a collective group of believers. Only then can we live out the authority He's given to the congregation.

Start

The church is the called-out people of God. But throughout the past two thousand years, people have often misunderstood the nature of the church—the reason for its existence, how it operates, and why it acts as it does. Too often we've accepted cartoonlike caricatures of the church to understand its nature.

> **As you begin this Bible study together with a group of other people, what do you hope to gain from learning about the nature and work of the church?**
>
> **What's the greatest blessing you've received from being part of a church?**

The church contains unity in diversity. As those who've confessed Christ as Lord and Savior, we now belong to the church. God doesn't require or expect us to leave our distinctiveness behind. Rather, He has a plan to work through each one of us. Yet He brings about a beautiful unity of faith amid the diversity of our individual lives.

The church requires that we work together but not by our own power or authority. Rather, God gives the people of God a kind of authority. It's a sacred trust that we must use wisely and only for God's glory. Let's see what Pastor Mark Dever has to say in video session 1 about God's intention for the church to exercise gospel authority in its work. Mark is the senior pastor of Capitol Hill Baptist Church in Washington, D.C.

Pray for God to open your hearts and minds before you watch the video for session 1.

Watch

Jesus intended us not to live the Christian life alone.

Elders have the responsibility to teach, to guide, but they aren't the church. The congregation is the church.

The elders are the steering wheel of the church. The congregation doesn't steer. The congregation is more like the emergency brake.

The congregation that sits and listens to false teaching bears some of the responsibility for that false teaching.

When you take that church covenant, you're taking it with all the members of that congregation.

The church is Jesus' evangelism plan, and it's also His discipleship plan.

In some sense the local church is like an assurance-of-salvation cooperative. We join because we want to help make sure we're following the Lord.

Discuss

Pastor Mark Dever said the church is both universal (meaning all true Christians in all churches at all times) and local (meaning a particular congregation of Christians).

Describe the way your congregation works together for God's glory.

Read aloud Acts 2:41-47.

What's the job of a congregation?

The congregation gathers to do certain activities. Baptism and the Lord's Supper are two of these activities. Pastor Mark also mentioned such things as preaching, hearing the Word, singing, and praying. But the role of the congregation is also to guard the gospel and the gospel people. More specifically, its job is to makes disciples and to guard the church against false teachers.

A key question we must ask about the work of the church is "Who leads in these practices?" How would you answer this question?

An important component of congregational authority is to call out leaders to lead out in areas of ministry. The congregation holds this authority as a body so that individuals don't become enamored with power and attempt to supplant Jesus' place as our sovereign Lord.

How should the church choose the people who hold offices?

The church is led by pastors and elders who are accountable to the congregation. The leaders are required to deliver the truth of the gospel to the congregation. In response the congregation must unify around sound doctrine and live out biblical faith.

Read aloud 2 Timothy 4:2-4.

> **What would cause a congregation to want their ears tickled rather than to hear the truth of Scripture?**

The apostle Paul was teaching Timothy, the pastor of a local congregation, about the dangers that would arise in ministry. False doctrine of the world is always a temptation for the church.

> **When the truth isn't taught by the church, who bears the weight of responsibility—the leaders or the congregation? Explain.**

Pastor Mark described the congregation as an emergency brake and the leadership as a steering wheel. These images help us understand congregational authority. The elders or pastors are responsible for guiding the church to learn God's Word and to be obedient to His mission. The congregation is responsible for confronting members and leaders who fall into false doctrine or become disobedient to Christ.

> **How does congregational authority facilitate evangelism?**

> **What's the congregation's role in discipleship?**

The congregation as a whole—not just individuals—establishes the proclamation of the gospel and then declares who has honestly responded in faith to that message. Rather than sending out lone-ranger Christians into the world, God accomplishes His evangelistic work through the church as it professes the gospel. Likewise, the church disciples believers. The whole church is responsible for this work.

Pray

As you reflect on the video teaching and the group discussion, you have an opportunity to pray for your church in specific ways. Here are some prayer priorities to focus on before the next group session.

- Unity in the life of your church, particularly in places where you have nothing in common but the gospel

- A culture of discipling in your church in which making and growing disciples is practiced as an ordinary part of the Christian life

- Discernment and faithfulness for elders and pastors in their work of leading the congregation to minister to one another

- Commitment to the work of the gospel in the church, recognizing the church's authority to protect and proclaim that gospel

- Faithfulness and repentance for members who are apathetic and content to remain anonymous in the life of the church

Prayer Requests

This Week's Plan

Worship

[ ] Read your Bible. Complete the reading plan on page 20.

[ ] Spend time with God by engaging with the devotional experience on page 21.

[ ] Spend time in daily prayer for the church and the members of the group.

Personal Study

[ ] Read and interact with "Biblical Order for the Church" on page 22.

[ ] Read and interact with "Working Together" on page 26.

Application

[ ] Identify an area in your life where the church hasn't had much influence. Invite a small group of friends (perhaps from your Bible-study group) to begin holding you accountable in this area.

[ ] Memorize 1 Corinthians 15:3-4: "I passed on to you as most important what I also received: that Christ died for our sins according to the Scriptures, that He was buried, that He was raised on the third day according to the Scriptures."

[ ] Start a journal by recording different ways you benefit from the work of the church. Use it as a way to offer thanks to God for His kind work toward you through His body.

[ ] List five church members who need ministry. Determine how, over the next few weeks, you can provide ministry to them in such a way that they better understand the power of the gospel.

Did you miss the group session?
Video sessions available for purchase at *lifeway.com/basics*

19

Read

Read the following Scripture passages this week. Use the acronym HEAR and the space provided to record your thoughts or action steps.

Day 1: I Corinthians 12:12-31a

Day 2: Matthew 18:15-20

Day 3: Acts 2:41-47

Day 4: Acts 4:32-37

Day 5: 2 Corinthians 6:14—7:1

Day 6: Matthew 16:13-19

Day 7: I Timothy 3:1-7

Reflect

LIVING AS PRIEST-KINGS OF THE KINGDOM

Christians are united with Christ. It's an overwhelming thought for mere mortals. As simple creatures who are born with a nature bent toward sin, we actively pursue rebellion. Yet through God's salvation we're transformed. God changes our identity from people who groped in the darkness. Now we're people who live by the light of Christ. Peter described our new identity. He said we're "a chosen race, a royal priesthood, a holy nation, a people for His possession" (1 Pet. 2:9). This verse helps us see who we are in Christ so that we can operate together in the congregational authority God gives us.

WE'RE A CHOSEN RACE. God knew we could never attain salvation for ourselves, so He extended His grace to us. By God's mercy Christians are plucked out of the condemnation we earned by our sin. Believers now make up a new chosen race that's distinct from the world.

WE'RE ROYAL PRIESTS. As God's adopted children, we possess authority to call others under His reign.

WE'RE A HOLY NATION. Collectively, we hold one another accountable for living out the faith. Not merely an intellectual exercise, holiness must occur in the daily grind. As fellow disciples, we help one another through counsel and ministry.

WE'RE OWNED BY GOD. His ownership over our lives and those in our church signifies an eternal shift. We're no longer slaves to sin. Instead, we serve the one true God. The Lord can now work in and through us to exercise His authority in the church.

In all these ways we publicly declare that God is the One—the only One—who can call us out of the darkness and into the light of His salvation.

Personal Study 1

BIBLICAL ORDER FOR THE CHURCH

Scripture gives some insight on the order of the church—the way the church governs itself. As Christians, we shouldn't see the order and leadership of our church as matters for others to decide. Instead, because we're part of God's people, we should be deeply concerned that the church operates as God intends. The authority of a congregation is expressed in the way it operates.

The New Testament calls for elders or pastors to oversee the church. (*Elder* and *pastor* are used interchangeably throughout this study.) The Bible also calls for the congregation's members to carry out the work of the church (see Eph. 4:12). Through this partnership between elders and members, a structure is established through which decisions are made. By engaging together, the elders and the members accomplish the work of gospel ministry. This type of church structure is often called elder-led congregationalism.

Elder-led congregationalism requires elders to lead and teach the members of the church their responsibilities for living as Christian disciples. As leaders, the elders are to focus their attention on two primary tasks: making decisions and training disciples.

> **Read Ephesians 4:11-16. How does the role of elders in a congregation ensure that the church remains faithful to God's mission?**

In *Understanding the Congregation's Authority* Jonathan Leeman states, "Elder-led congregationalism is a gospel powerhouse."[1] He describes five ways this form of church structure encourages a proper biblical order in a congregation, that is, the way the church is to carry out its mission.

1. GUARDS THE GOSPEL. The most important authority the church has is to declare and thereby guard the message of the gospel. Paul wrote:

> I am amazed that you are so quickly turning away from Him who called you by the grace of Christ and are turning to a different gospel—not that there is another gospel, but there are some who are troubling you and want to change the good news about the Messiah. But even if we or an angel from heaven should preach to you a gospel other than what we have preached to you, a curse be on him! As we have said before, I now say again: If anyone preaches to you a gospel contrary to what you received, a curse be on him!
> **Galatians 1:6-9**

Who in this passage is Paul tasking with protecting the gospel in the church—the members or the leaders? Why is this significant?

Paul gave the congregation more authority than even an apostle or an angel from heaven to protect the gospel message. This makes it important for church members to take seriously the task of learning, studying, and growing in their understanding of the gospel. A good pastor should always say, "Fire me if I begin to preach a false gospel," just as Paul did.

Read I Corinthians 15:1-11 and record a brief definition of *gospel.*

Overseeing the good news of Christ isn't given to Christian seminaries, missions agencies, or charities. It isn't given to philosophers, governors, or earthly rulers. Rather, it's entrusted to the leaders and members of a congregation to carefully tell and explain the gospel.

How does your church work to guard the gospel?

2. MATURES CHRISTIAN DISCIPLES.

2. MATURES CHRISTIAN DISCIPLES. A second result of biblical order in the church is that we fulfill our mission of making and maturing Christian disciples. The Great Commission states:

> All authority has been given to Me in heaven and on earth. Go, therefore, and make disciples of all nations, baptizing them in the name of the Father and of the Son and of the Holy Spirit, teaching them to observe everything I have commanded you. And remember, I am with you always, to the end of the age.
> **Matthew 28:18-20**

Circle the key words, especially the verbs, in the previous passage.

This commission comes from the lips of Jesus after His resurrection from the dead. He commanded us to go, make disciples, baptize, and teach. Notice that He didn't command us to make converts. Instead, we're to make disciples who join the church and mature in their love for and obedience to Christ.

3. STRENGTHENS THE WHOLE CHURCH. When the church ministers in the order set out by the New Testament, more people are able to participate. The whole church needs to be strengthened in its work. We miss the point of passages such as I Corinthians 12–14 when we reserve ministry for a select few. Instead, the Holy Spirit has placed gifts in the body of Christ as He wills, and each person has a role to play. Therefore, we should work—yes, work—to strengthen everyone.

4. FORTIFIES THE CHURCH'S HOLY INTEGRITY & WITNESS. When was the last time you heard or saw a positive story about a Christian congregation in the news? It happens but not very often. Knowing this would be the case, Jesus spoke about it in Matthew 5:10-12; 24:9; and John 15:18-25. Because we know persecution will happen, we must prepare one another for it.

A properly ordered church strengthens one another against the temptations of apathy and compromise. Dutifully strengthening one another makes it natural to challenge and uphold one another when temptation is near.

Record a time when another Christian held you accountable in a loving fashion to maintain your gospel integrity.

5. EQUIPS THE CONGREGATION TO LOVE ITS NEIGHBORS BETTER IN WORD AND DEED.
The church works to bring in others who will live as Christian disciples. It's the loving thing to do. We give a verbal witness so that others can know the truth and respond to it. We live out the commands of the Bible through our ministry so that others can see the impact of the gospel on our lives. Living in the congregation's authority enables believers to do these things more effectively.

In John 13:34-35 Jesus taught that the world will know we're Christians by our love for one another. Later in the New Testament James described the way we should live out our faith:

> Pure and undefiled religion before our God and Father is this: to look after orphans and widows in their distress and to keep oneself unstained by the world.
> **James 1:27**

James instructed us to care for those who can't care for themselves.

List ways your congregation can equip members to love the people of your community through both verbal witness and caring ministry.

As you close out this section, describe how biblical order enables the church to operate as God intends.

1. Jonathan Leeman, *Understanding the Congregation's Authority* (Nashville: B&H Publishing Group, 2016), 10.

Personal Study 2

WORKING TOGETHER

The church works together. That's God's plan for us. Consider the several images the New Testament uses for the church. Believers are pictured as the body of Christ (see 1 Cor. 12), a holy nation (see 1 Pet. 2:9), and a building not built by human hands (see 2 Cor. 5:1). God clearly positions His people as those who work together toward common goals for His kingdom.

> **Read 1 Corinthians 12:12-20. Record a summary of the passage to describe how the church works together.**

The church is designed to operate in such a way that it expresses the gospel and draws people to live by faith in Christ. This must happen within the biblical order that's brought about when the congregation expresses its spiritual authority. The church is Jesus' program for extending His reign throughout humanity. He's actively calling people to follow Him as both Lord and Savior. To do so, God has assembled Christian disciples together as the church. The way the church is organized and expresses its authority should fulfill the purpose for its existence.

Biblical order doesn't call for a small group to hold such power over the people that this leadership pack usurps the authority of Christ. Nor does it give us a system by which every member should feel the need to reset the course and strategy of the church. Paul told us that Jesus is "the head of the church" (Eph. 5:23). The church has elders leading under the headship of Jesus and members working in their spiritual authority to introduce the gospel to the world.

The Authority of the Body of Christ

Jesus once described the authority given to the congregation as "the keys of the kingdom" (Matt. 16:19). This concept has struck some people as mysterious, but placed in its context, it can be clearly understood.

Jesus was in Caesarea Philippi with His disciples when they discussed His identity according to the crowds and the apostles. Some of the crowds thought He was an Old Testament prophet who'd come back to life. When Jesus asked the apostles for their thoughts, Simon Peter stated his belief that Jesus is the Messiah, God's Son. Jesus clearly affirmed Peter's assertion:

> Jesus responded, "Simon son of Jonah, you are blessed because flesh and blood did not reveal this to you, but My Father in heaven. And I also say to you that you are Peter, and on this rock I will build My church, and the forces of Hades will not overpower it. I will give you the keys of the kingdom of heaven, and whatever you bind on earth is already bound in heaven, and whatever you loose on earth is already loosed in heaven."
> **Matthew 16:17-19**

Jesus was clear that the church is His to build. On our own we don't have the authority to do so. But then He made it equally clear that He would build the church on confessors who confess the right confession—that Jesus is the Christ, the Messiah.

Later, in Matthew 18:15-17, Jesus gave an additional teaching that helps us understand the authority that comes through "the keys of the kingdom of heaven" (Matt. 16:19). Believers are expected to hold fellow Christians accountable for living holy lives that reflect the gospel. If they don't repent, we're to lovingly challenge and correct them, even to the point of removing them from the fellowship of the church if they remain in sinful rebellion. The point in giving the collective church this authority is to identify what's a proper confession of the gospel and who's a proper confessor. We must discipline our communication of the gospel to be strictly biblical. Then we're to carefully identify who is and who isn't a member of the church. We bring in those who confess the gospel, and we remove those who won't live according to that confession.

How can a local congregation practically minister in a way
that shows they're using the keys of the kingdom?

The Work of Elders and Pastors

Let's briefly look at areas of the work that church leaders must accomplish
in elder-led congregational government.

ELDERS MUST LEAD. Hebrews 13:17 tells the church to obey its leaders.
Elders must study the Scriptures to understand how God intends for the
church to minister. On the other hand, leaders must not operate in a relational
vacuum. Instead, elders participate in a virtuous cycle of decision making
and building relationships. They lead congregational members as fellow
believers rather than lording over them like earthly dictators.

ELDERS MUST TEACH. When Paul wrote to Timothy about the qualifications for elders, he included the ability to teach (see 1 Tim. 3:2). Elders must
teach the congregation to live out the faith. They must also train those who will
later serve as elders. The men God calls and the congregation then recognizes as
elders must learn how to possess and exercise authority in the congregation.

Describe ways you can help the pastor or elders of your church
fulfill their responsibilities.

The Work of the Congregation

As a member of the congregation, you're a priest-king. Jonathan Leeman defines
this term this way: "If a king rules, a priest-king rules on behalf of a greater
king, God. That is, the priest-king mediates God's rule and works to protect
what's holy."[1] Under the new covenant of salvation through Christ, Christians
are set apart as the people of God. Our union with the true King—Jesus—gives

us the responsibility to declare God's rulership on the earth. Here are some practical ways church members can live out the faith as priest-kings.

ATTEND CHURCH REGULARLY. We're to faithfully assemble with the church (see Heb. 10:24-25). We need the encouragement and challenge of being with other believers. Additionally, they need our presence. Christians should see attending worship, Bible studies, and member meetings as important priorities.

HELP PRESERVE THE GOSPEL. The gospel is the primary truth that creates the church. In Galatians 3:1-5 Paul expressed his disappointment with the church in Galatia for being so quickly distracted from the gospel. As a congregational member, keep your mind and heart focused on communicating the gospel to the world.

HELP AFFIRM GOSPEL CITIZENS. By preserving the gospel message, we can know who is and who isn't suited to be affirmed as a member of the body of Christ. We do this not from malice but from kindness. It's the way churches know how to properly encourage a person toward Christlikeness. By affirming Christians as gospel citizens, we can disciple them toward maturity. Conversely, we can discipline those who are living counter to the gospel.

SHARE THE GOSPEL WITH OUTSIDERS. We're called to make disciples of all nations. According to 2 Corinthians 5:20, we're to "plead on Christ's behalf, 'Be reconciled to God.' " Exercising our authority isn't just for the interior work of church life. It's to declare the authority of the gospel to a world in rebellion. By doing so, we serve as priest-kings who are ambassadors of God and advocates for others to come under His good kingship.

> As you consider the work of the congregation, identify the area you need to work on most. Why did you identify this area?

1. Jonathan Leeman, *Understanding the Congregation's Authority* (Nashville: B&H Publishing Group, 2016), 21.

Baptism and the Lord's Supper

Week 2

When the church worships, we declare that God is great. Collectively, we celebrate both God's character and His work in the world. The church's worship is a central focus for us as individual believers. By participating in worship, we connect to the larger family of faith. Rather than standing to the side and viewing worship or missing out altogether, we affirm that we're part of the people of the Christian faith.

Congregational worship ought to contain biblical elements, such as reading Scripture, singing in worship, and listening to sermons that explain the Word of God. In all of these practices, the church must prioritize the good news of Jesus Christ.

This week we'll study two practices of the church: baptism and the Lord's Supper. Many congregations refer to these as the ordinances of the church.

By participating in these ordinances, believers proclaim their individual faith in the gospel. And because the church as a whole practices them, these ordinances serve as specific ways a congregation affirms believers' professions and preaches the gospel to one another and to the world.

Start

Welcome everyone to session 2 of *Basics*.

Use the following content to begin your time together.

The church's worship includes some expected things. We sing, hear a sermon, pray, and encourage one another. Hopefully, no matter what action takes place, a local church emphasizes the gospel at each gathering. It's the central message for us as Christians.

> **In your church's recent worship services how have you seen
> the gospel presented as the congregation's primary message?**

The practices, or ordinances, of baptism and the Lord's Supper occur at different intervals in the life of a church, depending on the congregation to which you belong. Some churches observe the Lord's Supper each week, while others may do so quarterly. Congregations generally practice baptism after candidates profess faith in Christ. These two practices have been around for thousands of years. Baptism predates the ministry of Jesus. The Lord's Supper was instituted by Christ Himself.

> **How could ignoring baptism and the Lord's Supper harm
> the church's witness for the gospel?**

In this session H. B. Charles Jr. will guide us to better understand the nature of these two ancient practices. In discussing them as a group, you'll see that they have great application to the life of today's church. H. B. is the pastor-teacher at Shiloh Metropolitan Baptist Church in Jacksonville, Florida.

Pray for God to open your hearts and minds before you watch the video for session 2.

Watch

Use the space below to follow along and take notes as you watch video session 2.

Baptism and the Lord's Supper

1. These are Christian essentials.
2. These are biblical commands.
3. These are symbols of salvation.

Baptism identifies us with the death, burial, and resurrection of the Lord Jesus Christ.

The practice of the Lord's Supper is an ongoing practice to constantly remind both the individual believer and the corporate body that we are saved in the relationship with God and one another on the basis of what Christ has done for us, not what we do for Him.

The practice of baptism is not only a means of identifying us with Christ, but it identifies us with Christ and the church.

Baptism is the way the believer declares, "Jesus is Lord" and identifies himself as a part of the new community of Christ and the kingdom of God.

How to Prepare Your Heart for the Lord's Supper

1. The process begins on the part of pastors and church leaders.
2. Be present.
3. Come to the table with clean hands.

The coming of the Lord's Supper is a call for us to repent and to confess and to forgive and be reconciled so that our hearts are ready to honor the Lord.

These are high, celebrative moments because these are the silent sermons of the church. Without words they illustrate what it means to be saved in Jesus Christ.

When you are dealing with baptism and the Lord's Supper, you are dealing with ground zero of the Christian faith. This is the epicenter of what we believe.

Discuss

Use the following statements and questions to discuss the video.

Pastor H. B. Charles Jr. explained that the ordinances of baptism and the Lord's Supper are too often neglected in the church today. In fact, he said, "These are Christian essentials. ... These are biblical commands."

In what ways is baptism an essential part of the Christian life?

For the church to know who's declaring Christ as their Lord, there must be a public statement about it. Otherwise, we're all just attendees at religious gatherings. Jesus' intent was that we would confess our faith in Him before humankind in some way.

Read aloud Matthew 28:18-20.

What's the meaning of baptism?

Explain why baptism isn't a private act but should be done publicly before the church.

How does baptism mark you as a member of the church?

The Lord's Supper was begun, of course, by the Lord Jesus. We find its origin in Matthew 26:17-30 and Luke 22:1-39. Later the apostle Paul warned against any abuses of this ordinance in I Corinthians 11:17-34. Paul's command to the Corinthian church was for people to carefully examine themselves before partaking of the Lord's Supper. We shouldn't knowingly carry sin into the observance.

Read aloud Luke 22:17-20.

What does the Lord's Supper cause us to remember?

These two ordinances tie us to Christ and His church. When we engage with them, we identify with the church that belongs to Jesus because these practices declare His good news. When we practice them, we have an opportunity to be thankful for what He has done for us in the gospel.

The gospel should be at the root of all our congregation's work. About baptism and the Lord's Supper, Pastor H. B. Charles Jr. said, "You are dealing with ground zero of the Christian faith." By collectively engaging in the ordinances, we identify with and declare the gospel to the world.

In the week leading up to the Lord's Supper, how should church members prepare to receive it?

The church is to practice these ordinances because they were given to the church, and only the church has the authority to affirm professions of faith in the gospel. Therefore, church leaders and members worship together through them.

Should baptism and the Lord's Supper be practiced with a solemn attitude or with a celebrative spirit? Explain your answers.

Pray

As you reflect on the video teaching and the group discussion, you have an opportunity to pray for your church in specific ways. Here are some prayer priorities to focus on before the next group session.

- Unity amid diversity in the life of your church, especially that members will engage with one another for the gospel's sake across ethnic, economic, and educational lines

- That members of the church will be deliberate about sharing the gospel and that we'll see conversions

- Trust in the power of God's Word for the preaching pastor as he preaches every week

- Clarity for those who plan the church's worship services

- For unbelievers to turn to Jesus in repentance and faith

- For Christians to faithfully observe the Lord's Supper

Prayer Requests

This Week's Plan

Worship

[ ] Read your Bible. Complete the reading plan on page 38.

[ ] Spend time with God by engaging with the devotional experience on page 39.

[ ] Spend time in daily prayer for the church and the members of the group.

Personal Study

[ ] Read and interact with "What Baptism Accomplishes" on page 40.

[ ] Read and interact with "Observing the Lord's Supper" on page 44.

Application

[ ] Record your baptism testimony. Create a document that tells your story of coming to faith in Christ so that you can easily learn how to share it.

[ ] Memorize Romans 6:4: "We were buried with Him by baptism into death, in order that, just as Christ was raised from the dead by the glory of the Father, so we too may walk in a new way of life."

[ ] Add to your journal by recording an experience from the most recent observance of the Lord's Supper in your church. Take time to reflect on its meaning in your life.

[ ] Reach out to a friend who hasn't been baptized. Pray beforehand and prepare yourself to share the gospel and the meaning of baptism.

Did you miss the group session?
Video sessions available for purchase at *lifeway.com/basics*

37

Read

Read the following Scripture passages this week. Use the acronym HEAR and the space provided to record your thoughts or action steps.

Day 1: Acts 8:26-40

Day 2: Romans 6:1-11

Day 3: I Corinthians 11:17-26

Day 4: I Corinthians 11:27-34

Day 5: Matthew 26:26-35

Day 6: Matthew 3:13-17

Day 7: I Corinthians 10:14-22

Reflect

GATHERING FOR WORSHIP

Worship is one of the primary activities of the church. A good and necessary part of your personal devotion to Christ includes worship as a daily activity. But the Bible also clearly teaches that we're to gather with other believers regularly for the purpose of worship.

In Ephesians 5 Paul taught the early church to be filled with the Holy Spirit. When they would do so, they would find themselves "speaking to one another in psalms, hymns, and spiritual songs, singing and making music from [their] heart[s] to the Lord" (v. 19). When Christians submit to the Holy Spirit's power in their lives, worship will be the result.

The church worships together to make a declaration. Our declaration is, first, heavenward. Congregational members set aside time that could have been devoted to worldly pursuits in order to direct our collective attention to God.

When we worship, we also minister. As we set our hearts aside for God's praise, we better understand His purposes for the church. Hebrews 10:24-25 identifies one of those purposes:

> Let us be concerned about one another in order to promote love and good works, not staying away from our worship meetings, as some habitually do, but encouraging each other, and all the more as you see the day drawing near.
> **Hebrews 10:24-25**

Our worship of God should lead to public ministry. Our praise of Jesus declares that His gospel has the power to save and sanctify. Therefore, as we move from worship into the world, the impact of the gospel should become immediately evident in our lives.

Personal Study 1

WHAT BAPTISM ACCOMPLISHES

Baptism should be a regular occurrence in the life of a congregation. But there's nothing that should be commonplace about it. Baptism is a public declaration about an eternal reality. It's important for a local church body to treat it with importance.

What level of importance is placed on baptism in your church?

When there's a baptism in your church's worship service, what's the normal response of the congregation?

Baptism is an ordinance of the church. The word *ordinance* refers to a practice that demonstrates a believer's faith. We don't use the word *sacrament,* as other faith traditions do, because that word is sometimes associated with the idea of dispensing grace. We believe grace is given not through human works but only through work done by God. Then why should we focus so much attention on baptism? There are several reasons. Baptism plays an important role in helping us confess our faith and become a vital member of the church.

Baptism Allows You to Confess Your Faith

After we place our faith in Christ for salvation, we should declare our faith publicly. Our salvation isn't something to be held secretly. It's a total change of our eternal destiny. Salvation from Jesus Christ transfers a person from the darkness into the light of God's kingdom (see 1 Pet. 2:9). Salvation brings about a spiritual transformation that should be noticeable to everyone.

Part of shedding the light of God's kingdom in the world is publicly professing our faith in Jesus. The early believers were commanded to do so. In Acts 2:38-41 Peter preached at Pentecost shortly following Jesus' ascension to heaven. Peter told the crowd to put their faith in Christ for salvation and then be baptized (see v. 38). Baptism isn't done to somehow complete our salvation. If we believe Jesus needs our help, then we don't believe the true gospel. Instead, baptism is a public confession that we've been saved.

Does this sound similar to your own understanding of baptism? Why or why not?

If by faith you've trusted Christ as your Savior and you haven't been baptized, what's holding you back?

The ordinance of baptism is highlighted in several other New Testament passages. Specifically, the apostle Paul wrote about the subject of baptism to the churches in Rome and Galatia.

Read Romans 6:3-4. How does the practice of baptism allow a Christian to identify with the death of Jesus Christ?

Read Galatians 3:25-27. What does the image of putting on Christ like a garment communicate?

People who've come into a saving relationship with Christ should see baptism as an honor and an opportunity. It allows those who've made their professions of faith in Christ to tell their friends and community about the power of the gospel to save.

Baptism Depicts the Gospel Message

The word *baptism* is usually translated as *immersion*. Before Philip baptized the Ethiopian eunuch in Acts 8, the Ethiopian said, "Look, there's water! What would keep me from being baptized?" (v. 36). In the following verses the scene describes Philip and the man going "down into the water" (v. 38). The method for immersing a professing Christian in water is a portrait of the entire gospel message. It represents the death and resurrection of Jesus Christ.

Read the following verses.

What should we say then? Should we continue in sin so that grace may multiply? Absolutely not! How can we who died to sin still live in it? Or are you unaware that all of us who were baptized into Christ Jesus were baptized into His death? Therefore we were buried with Him by baptism into death, in order that, just as Christ was raised from the dead by the glory of the Father, so we too may walk in a new way of life.
Romans 6:1-4

Using this passage, how would you explain the meaning of baptism to a new Christian?

Even the language we use when baptizing a Christian is important. In the Great Commission in Matthew 28:18-20, Jesus specified some of what we're to say. The church baptizes people "in the name of the Father and of the Son and of the Holy Spirit" (v. 19). This phrase shows that the power of salvation fully rests in God, not in our abilities or religious activities.

Baptism Allows You to Be Included in the Church

We often emphasize what the person being baptized is saying through baptism. But remember that baptism involves two parties, not just one. The person being baptized professes faith in Christ, while the church formally and publicly affirms that person's profession. Like the Lord's Supper, baptism isn't an individual event but a corporate event. It's when the church hands a professing Christian the team jersey: "You're with us now!" As such, baptism is a necessary prerequisite to membership in a church. Baptism symbolizes that the person is now a Christian and now belongs to the kingdom of God.

This is the reason baptism should ordinarily be administered in whole-church gatherings. The church is bearing a witness to the world that the recipients of baptism have moved their citizenship. They now belong to Christ and thus are part of the church.

Baptism Is an Opportunity for Evangelism

When the church gathers, we should invite non-Christians to witness our worship. It's an opportunity for them to hear the Word taught and to learn of their need for God's salvation. In addition, the ordinance of baptism is a powerful way for a new Christian to declare everyone's need for salvation.

Too often church members have the misconception that gospel proclamation is reserved only for the preaching pastor. Not so. When people give their public professions of faith through baptism, they participate in the evangelism of the lost. Baptism isn't done just to check off a box on a religious do-and-don't list. It's an opportunity to show and share the good news.

When the elders or pastors administer baptism, it verbally and visually declares our need for salvation. It's therefore wise for new Christians and members of the church to invite the lost to be present for the ordinance. As baptism takes place, a personal testimony is given, and the gospel is explained.

What can your congregation do to make sure the practice of baptism fulfills an evangelistic purpose?

Personal Study 2

OBSERVING THE LORD'S SUPPER

The church has observed the Lord's Supper throughout its entire history. Through the ages it's been known by various names and practiced in various ways. For our purposes in this study, the term *Lord's Supper* will be used.

Throughout history the Lord's Supper has often been misunderstood. In the early days of the church, some citizens of the Roman Empire perceived that Christians were cannibals. After all, the teaching included a meal that centered on body and blood. That's always been an easily dispelled myth. Some have held and some still hold that the Lord's Supper dispenses God's grace. Again, the Lord's Supper is best understood as an ordinance instead of a sacrament. As a symbol and visible representation of the gospel, the practice doesn't have any power to transfer God's power to a person.

Why is it important to understand the Lord's Supper only as a way to communicate or symbolize the gospel?

Coming Together

In many congregations today the Lord's Supper is offered as a personal statement of our faith in Christ Jesus and as a corporate affirmation of our oneness in Him (see I Cor. 10:17). Knowing what the ordinance represents, the church should include it in its congregational gatherings.

First Corinthians 10:16-17; 11:17-34 are the most extensive passages on the Lord's Supper in the Bible. Paul's teachings read as if the early Christians partook of the ordinance during an actual meal. This would make sense because the Lord's Supper has a theological connection to the Passover meal practiced by the Jews for several thousand years. Verses 33-34 make it clear that hospitality and deference should be shown to one another when observing a meal.

How would seeing the practice of the Lord's Supper in connection with a meal be helpful in understanding its meaning?

The Lord's Supper is a congregational activity. It's another way the whole church makes a declaration about who has entered God's kingdom and who hasn't. Participation in the Lord's Supper is a means by which the whole church declares the need of Christ's sacrifice for our salvation. It's something we do together. Therefore, individual participants in the ordinance should have already made personal declarations of faith in Christ.

We can summarize the declaration the church makes in the Lord's Supper by looking in four directions: backward, inward, outward, and forward.

Looking Backward

The Lord's Supper looks back to the work of Jesus on our behalf. Paul's instructions to the Corinthian church mirror the words of Jesus at the last supper. Paul instructed the Corinthian church in a similar manner:

> I received from the Lord what I also passed on to you: On the night when He was betrayed, the Lord Jesus took bread, gave thanks, broke it, and said, "This is My body, which is for you. Do this in remembrance of Me." In the same way, after supper He also took the cup and said, "This cup is the new covenant established by My blood. Do this, as often as you drink it, in remembrance of Me."
> **1 Corinthians 11:23-25**

If Jesus is your Lord, record your testimony of how His sacrifice provided your salvation.

The idea of remembering is common in the Bible. God often commanded the people of Israel to remember His work for them. They were to remember events like the times when the Lord delivered them from slavery in Egypt, gave them the law, and created the covenant with Abraham. As the church, we should focus our spiritual minds to remember the work of Jesus.

What you can do to intentionally recall and celebrate God's work on your behalf?

Looking Inward

Whoever eats the bread or drinks the cup of the Lord in an unworthy way will be guilty of sin against the body and blood of the Lord. So a man should examine himself; in this way he should eat the bread and drink from the cup. For whoever eats and drinks without recognizing the body, eats and drinks judgment on himself. This is why many are sick and ill among you, and many have fallen asleep. If we were properly evaluating ourselves, we would not be judged, but when we are judged, we are disciplined by the Lord, so that we may not be condemned with the world.
1 Corinthians 11:27-32

Some may look at this passage and feel that Paul was being too harsh. In fact, however, he's helping us guard one another from falling into punishment. When we take part in the Lord's Supper, we collectively and individually declare that Jesus is our Lord. If we treated such a practice lightly, we would deserve for God to judge us harshly.

Reread the passage and underline the steps we should take to ensure that we participate in a worthy manner.

Maybe you're wondering why God treats this ordinance so seriously. Reading the rest of the New Testament doesn't yield any similar teachings about other components of our worship. God takes the Lord's Supper seriously because He takes Jesus' sacrifice so seriously. To treat the observance like a humdrum religious activity would insult Jesus' death for our sin. Therefore, God requires the church and its individual members to carefully examine our hearts before we take the Lord's Supper.

Paul commands us to search our hearts for sin. In this examination we once again have the opportunity to encounter God's mercy and grace. The entire Lord's Supper experience gives the church an opportunity to declare that although we're sinful, Christ's sacrifice is sufficient for our redemption.

What are ways you can examine your heart in preparation for observing the Lord's Supper?

Looking Outward

> The cup of blessing that we give thanks for, is it not a sharing in the blood of Christ? The bread that we break, is it not a sharing in the body of Christ? Because there is one bread, we who are many are one body, for all of us share that one bread.
> **1 Corinthians 10:16-17**

We as a church are one body. How do we know? We know "because there is one bread" (v. 16). In other words, taking the Lord's Supper isn't a private act. It's not an event a father should do with his children at home or for a couple in a wedding service. It's a church act. It's a church-revealing act.

Looking Forward

The Lord's Supper is also a way we look toward the future. Paul wrote, "As often as you eat this bread and drink the cup, you proclaim the Lord's death until He comes" (1 Cor. 11:26). When we partake of the Lord's Supper, we can look forward to Jesus' future return to complete His work of restoration. This forward-looking posture gives the church an urgency to make disciples. Even though the Lord's Supper is an intimate time of examination and celebration, it isn't something to be held in secret. Rather, it's a witness we can share with unbelievers that the return of Christ is imminent.

How can you help others understand the gospel through the Lord's Supper?

Stewardship

The subject of money can be an emotional issue for people. It's often considered to be intensely private, and discussing our finances in public seems inappropriate to many people.

Our reticence about financial matters is likely due to the fact that the way we use money says a great deal about the state of our heart. It's no wonder, then, that the Bible addresses the issue of money on numerous occasions. When we study the Scriptures, we're introduced to the idea of serving as a good steward, or manager, of our money.

God requires that we properly care for what He's entrusted to us. But stewardship isn't just an individual activity. Churches receive tithes and offerings from their members in order to do God's kingdom work in the community. But stewardship is more than just the financial ability to do good work. It's a sign of faith by the members of the church.

In this session we'll look to Scripture to learn some ways the church leads people to be good stewards and collectively lives out the principles of good stewardship.

Start

Welcome everyone to session 3 of *Basics*.

Use the following content to begin your time together.

The subject of money can be an emotional issue. At work we hide our salary figures. Homeowners-association meetings can get heated over discussions of how to spend the annual dues. Even in our own homes we can become agitated with one another about ways money is saved and spent.

How well are you doing in the area of generosity?

As members of the church, we're called to carry out ministry together. Membership in the church is more than just having your name on a roster. It means you've placed your life in a covenant relationship with Jesus and His people. So we spend our time together in discipleship, worship, and missionary endeavors for the gospel.

In this covenant we're pledging to obey God in everything He requires of us and to do it together. Here's where the idea of stewardship becomes pivotal. Stewardship recognizes that we don't own what's in our hands. Rather, we're the managers.

In this session we'll investigate what the Bible has to say about stewardship, not just individually but collectively as the church. Let's listen to Pastor Vance H. Pitman discuss a biblical view of stewardship as foundational to the life of the church. Vance is the senior pastor of Hope Church in Las Vegas, Nevada.

Pray for God to open your hearts and minds before you watch the video for session 3.

Watch

Use the space below to follow along and take notes as you watch video session 3.

The Biblical Principles of Stewardship

1. It all belongs to Him.
2. He's entrusted some of that to me.
3. It's my responsibility to manage what belongs to Him.

Giving is stewarding what already belongs to Him in such a way that it honors Him and advances His kingdom and accomplishes His mission.

You and I are really never more like Jesus than when we're giving.

We value living life ready to make a difference in the lives of others.

We don't give to a church. We give through a church as an investment in the kingdom of God.

What the Bible Says About Stewardship

1. Give to the Lord.
2. Save for the future.
3. Budget to live.

What the Bible Says About Giving

1. Always a portion
2. Sometimes a sacrifice

When I gain, I'm to always, regularly, systematically give a portion of that to the Lord.

There are times and seasons when God calls us to give sacrificially.

Discuss

Stewardship is a term the church uses to indicate that we're managers of God's possessions. In his church Pastor Vance H. Pitman reminds the congregation that God owns everything but entrusts some of His resources to us.

> **What difference does it make in your attitude toward tithing and stewardship when you recognize God's ownership of all things?**

> **What are the things in life with which you have the most trouble being generous?**

Pastor Vance stated that giving is a standard practice we see throughout the Bible. Abraham gave tithes. The law God gave through Moses to the Hebrew people included commands to tithe. We learn about giving generously through the Prophets, the teachings of Jesus, and the letters in the New Testament.

> **What do we learn about generosity by understanding that tithing was practiced before God gave the law to the Hebrew people?**

Biblical stewardship recognizes that God owns everything. Through that recognition we see that God doesn't have any need for what we fiscally hold in our bank accounts or physically hold as possessions. Because God doesn't need our stuff, He must have another reason for requiring us to give Him our offerings.

Read aloud Proverbs 3:9.

Discuss the impact on your spiritual life when you give from the firstfruits (from the top of what you earn) rather than from what's left over.

Our giving is another means by which we become like Christ. Rather than seeing giving as merely a way to fund church programs, we should realize its impact on our discipleship.

Read aloud John 3:16-17.

Describe the nature of God in giving His Son for our sin.

How is stewardship related to the gospel?

How does financial giving aid Christians in their discipleship?

Pastor Vance stated, "We don't give to a church. We give through a church." When we lack generosity, there's a problem in the way we view the mission of God. Though God doesn't need our finances, He uses them in the lives of local congregations and in world missions.

Read aloud Philippians 4:18-19.

How can an entire church model stewardship?

What should churches do with the finances they receive?

Pray

As you reflect on the video teaching and the group discussion, you have an opportunity to pray for your church in specific ways. Here are some prayer priorities to focus on before the next group session.

- Unity in the life of the church, particularly in using our finances to love one another

- For members to be faithful stewards in their personal lives

- Discernment and integrity by church leaders as they make plans for using the offerings given to the church

- Generosity with personal finances in ways that contribute to evangelistic opportunities

- For unbelievers to turn to Jesus in repentance and faith

Prayer Requests

This Week's Plan

Worship

[ ] Read your Bible. Complete the reading plan on page 56.

[ ] Spend time with God by engaging with the devotional experience on page 57.

[ ] Spend time in daily prayer for the church and the members of the group.

Personal Study

[ ] Read and interact with "Believers Give" on page 58.

[ ] Read and interact with "Congregations Give" on page 62.

Application

[ ] Assess your spending patterns over the past month. Determine whether you're faithfully giving to your church.

[ ] Memorize Matthew 6:21: "Where your treasure is, there your heart will be also."

[ ] Update your journal with a story about ways your church has been generous to people in need.

[ ] Personally connect with someone you know who's struggling financially and invite them over for a meal. Take time to pray with them at the meal.

Did you miss the group session?
Video sessions available for purchase at *lifeway.com/basics*

55

Read

Read the following Scripture passages this week. Use the acronym HEAR and the space provided to record your thoughts or action steps.

Day 1: 2 Corinthians 8

Day 2: I Corinthians 9:I4; I Timothy 5:I7-I8

Day 3: 2 Corinthians 9

Day 4: Acts 2:4I-47

Day 5: Malachi 3:7-I2

Day 6: Matthew 6:I9-24

Day 7: Proverbs 3:5-I9

Reflect

WHAT WE TREASURE

In Matthew 6:19-24 Jesus taught His disciples how they should treat their possessions. Take a moment and read the passage from your Bible.

As Christians, we must carefully choose our priorities in life. After all, if we don't choose priorities based on spiritual principles, our flesh will naturally seek the things of the world. Jesus' description of the temporary nature of earthly possessions sounds an alarm for us about where we place ultimate value. In the end earthly possessions, no matter how valuable, are all temporary. Everything here on earth has an expiration date.

Our culture has grown accustomed to these expiration dates and in some cases even looks forward to them. Just consider the media buzz every time a new smartphone, a computer-operating system, a car, or a change in fashion is introduced.

Jesus' teaching leads us to see that our heart's affections and our "treasure chest" are inseparable. Using the image of the eye as "the lamp of the body" (v. 22), our Lord shows us the danger of greed and envy. If we're consumed with what others possess, we invite darkness into our lives.

Instead, we need to choose the better of the two options we have to be our master. We can serve money, or we can serve Christ. It's impossible to have divided loyalties. Jesus said we'll love one and despise the other (see v. 24). It's a challenging idea. We never want to think we'd hate Jesus just because of the priority we place on our possessions. But that's the stark reality He presented.

You have a choice before you. Fully place your heart's affections and your mind's attention on Jesus. Then you'll enjoy the one treasure that can never fade away.

Personal Study 1

BELIEVERS GIVE

We live in a transactional society. We pay. We get. It should all work out evenly and fairly. But it rarely happens that way. The seller is trying to get paid top dollar, while the buyer is trying to save as much as possible.

In church life pastors are often reserved about speaking on the subject of money. The perception is that church members don't want to hear about a need for "more money" again and again. Yet the members who are deeply committed to the work and ministry of the church are happy for church leaders to address the issue. The culture's transactional attitude toward money shouldn't determine whether the church discusses this important issue.

> **From the choices below, circle how often the subject of money, stewardship, and generosity is addressed in your church.**
> **Never • Once a year • Multiple times a year • Every week**

Christians should be concerned about their personal financial stewardship for a very specific reason: the gospel. The Bible addresses giving in 2 Corinthians 8–9. As Paul discussed the work of the church and the individual's work of giving, he ended with this statement: "Thanks be to God for His indescribable gift" (2 Cor. 9:15). Paul wanted the believers to understand that the motivation for their giving as individual Christians and as a congregation was their response to God's gift of salvation. Unless this is the reason you give offerings, you'll quit in short order.

An Old Testament Teaching on Giving

In the final book of the Old Testament, the prophet Malachi confronted Judah for its sins against God and against one another. The nation was acting as a faithless people. One of its sins was the refusal to bring tithes to the temple. Because of this refusal, the people were acting immaturely in their spiritual lives and were jeopardizing the work of the temple for the poor.

Tithe literally means *a tenth of your income.* Old Testament laws stipulated that faithful Hebrews tithe and bring various offerings as part of their worship. The important issue today isn't the percentage of our giving but the reason for it.

Read Malachi 3:7-12. How were the people of God sinning?

Verse 7 deals with the subject of returning to God. What does our financial giving have to do with our faithfulness to God?

Verse 8 says the people were robbing God. Describe how the refusal to tithe is a form of robbery.

The call to biblical stewardship over our money is included in God's call to faithful living. Too often we think of our offerings as an outward act. However, giving isn't an activity of our bank accounts but of our hearts. Our offerings are a sign of our faith in God's goodness to us. Giving is an act that states God is the Lord of our lives. All we have and all we are belong to Him. In giving our finances, we state that we believe He's a good Ruler. So holding back from the financial generosity that He commands is going back on our own testimonies of God's lordship over us.

If you've fallen short in this arena of your life, there's good news: God forgives! Your generosity toward God can be renewed as it begins to reflect the generosity of His forgiveness.

The Proof of Faithfulness in Giving

James 2:26 reminds us that "faith without works is dead." Just as we trust in Christ for our eternal salvation, we can also trust the Lord for the daily provisions of our lives. Read God's words in Malachi 3:10:

> "Bring the full tenth into the storehouse so that there may be food in My
> house. Test Me in this way," says the LORD of Hosts. "See if I will not open
> the floodgates of heaven and pour out a blessing for you without measure."
> **Malachi 3:10**

The idea of testing the Lord is something we should treat carefully. It's not that we're going to make God do something in response to our work. Rather, we're acting in faith on His promise. As a result, we'll see the proof of God's faithfulness to us through our participation in His covenant activity.

When God speaks of the storehouse, He's referring to the ministry of His people in worship, to one another, and to the world. Giving to other charities, especially Christian ones, is a good thing to do. But none of those other organizations have been created by God as the church has.

New Testament Teachings on Giving

Jesus personally addressed the issue of possessions in His Sermon on the Mount (see Matt. 5–7). Throughout the passage Jesus addressed ways His disciples should live in and interact with the world.

Read Matthew 6:19-24, in which Jesus specifically addressed our possessions. Make a list of the ways worldly treasures will fail us.

Later in the Gospel of Matthew, as Jesus addressed the hypocrisy of the Pharisees, He pronounced this over them:

> Woe to you, scribes and Pharisees, hypocrites! You pay a
> tenth of mint, dill, and cumin, yet you have neglected the more
> important matters of the law—justice, mercy, and faith. These
> things should have been done without neglecting the others.
> Blind guides! You strain out a gnat, yet gulp down a camel!
> **Matthew 23:23-24**

Jesus didn't tell the Pharisees to stop giving their tithes. However, He instructed them not to neglect justice, mercy, and faith. Our tithing should go hand in hand with other essential components of gospel-centered living.

Jesus was clear that our giving is a sign of who or what our master is. In Matthew 6:24 He said we can't serve both Him and money.

Record the spiritual effects in each area when you serve money or God.

	MONEY	GOD
Work		
Marriage		
Evangelism		
Parenting		
Hobbies		

As Paul was departing from the church in Ephesus, he concluded his farewell with a statement about generosity:

> In every way I've shown you that by laboring like this, it is necessary to help the weak and to keep in mind the words of the Lord Jesus, for He said, "It is more blessed to give than to receive."
> **Acts 20:35**

As Christians, we should follow God's example. The Father gave His Son. The Son gave His life. When we're saved, we're given the presence of the Holy Spirit as a down payment for the eternal salvation we're inheriting. Our offerings are small in comparison to God's magnanimous work. But they're something we can give to mirror the beauty of the gospel's work for us.

Personal Study 2

CONGREGATIONS GIVE

As Paul wrote his second letter to the Corinthian church, he encouraged the believers to think beyond their own needs. As a church, they had the ability to bless, invest in, and make a difference for others.

> **Read 2 Corinthians 9:1-5. How would you describe this church's attitude toward giving?**

> **Why did Paul encourage the Corinthian church to have the right attitude about the offerings given to the congregation?**

Eager Giving

Paul emphasized the Corinthian church's eagerness to give and noted that its enthusiasm had spread to other congregations as well. But he didn't want the Corinthians to lose ground in their Christian maturity and become embarrassed if they were unprepared to give to the needs of others.

From this passage we learn that giving is an act of both faith and faithfulness. To supply for the needs of others, the Corinthian church would have to act in faith. It wasn't as if the congregation didn't have its own physical needs that required money. The church family needed food, shelter, and other provisions. But seeing the needs of the Macedonians, the believers in Corinth were willing to act in faith that God would continually supply for them.

Giving is also an act of faithfulness to God and the body of Christ. We should be obedient to God's call for us to be a generous people. As Jesus taught in Matthew 6, our loyalties can't be divided between God and money. Instead, the way we use our money must reflect our faithfulness as servants of Jesus and His gospel message.

We must also remain faithful to the church because we're all in the same spiritual family. We must continually care for one another by using our resources to meet one another's needs.

> **In which of the following ways is your church investing in ministry to others?**
> □ Supporting church plants in your city
> □ Supporting international and domestic missionaries
> □ Providing orphan care with gospel intentionality
> □ Caring for widows with gospel intentionality
> □ Aiding the poor as you witness of the gospel
> □ Participating in evangelistic ministries
> □ Supporting short-term mission trips
> □ Other:

Biological Realities

In 2 Corinthians 9:6-10 Paul used the image of sowing and reaping to help the church better understand why giving is so important. As churches, we face the temptation to create minifortresses in our church programming, spending all our resources on our own needs.

The offerings received from members of the congregation can be used for internal or external purposes, but we don't have to pit these two needs against each other. Yes, a local church needs to care for the needs of its members, but the church can also care for people and places that are in great need around the world and within its own community. Paul's image of planting seed and harvesting crops emphasizes the need to reach beyond the walls of the church.

Read 2 Corinthians 9:6-10. What kind of harvest is your church gaining from its sowing?

As God calls us to be faithful to our sowing (giving), then the question arises about the nature of our harvesting (reward).

As you've seen others' faithfulness in giving, what kinds of rewards have you seen in their lives?

Often we mistakenly believe if we give money, God will reward us monetarily. But God has a much greater reward in store for us. Read 2 Corinthians 9:8-13 and list the rewards that come from a church's generosity.

To receive a financial reward for our church's generosity is fine, but there's so much more that God wants us to receive. It begins with grace. God causes an overflow of grace to us when we release our grip on the money and things of this world (see v. 8). There's perhaps no greater return on our investment in ministry than to experience the grace of God.

We can also see in verse 8 that this grace from God includes an equipping element. A church's stewardship allows God's grace to prepare the members for future ministry work. By God's grace we can "excel in every good work."

In what different ways does your church plan and prepare members for the work of ministry?

How might teaching biblical stewardship do more to help
Christians engage in gospel work?

Profitable Giving

The idea of profit is tied to the economic principle that we retain more
than we spend. But the spiritual idea of profit is quite the opposite. Our
faith profits when we give away more than we can personally afford. This
is a way our lives can reflect the gospel.

The image of sowing and reaping shows us that what we keep is all we have—
the small seeds in our hand. But what we give away is used by God to
multiply the effects of ministry for the sake of the gospel. God uses this
principle to teach believers about the faith needed for giving and the results
that come from giving. Churches must embrace the same principle. In freely
giving to the needs of others, we display the heart of the gospel message.

The Old Testament prophet Malachi communicated this principle in his
address about tithing. In response to faithful giving and God's reward,
he wrote, " 'Then all the nations will consider you fortunate, for you will
be a delightful land,' says the LORD of Hosts" (Mal. 3:12). Paul expressed
the same idea in 2 Corinthians 9:13:

> They will glorify God for your obedience to the confession of the
> gospel of Christ, and for your generosity in sharing with them
> and with others through the proof provided by this service.
> **2 Corinthians 9:13**

The church can increase its gospel witness through generosity.
What ministries should your church engage in to better reveal
the gospel's message of God's gift of salvation?

Church Discipline

Week 4

"This is going to hurt me more than it's going to hurt you."

Have you ever heard parents say this? You may have had parents who said this to you. What did they mean by this? Well, it's likely they were acknowledging the unpleasantries of discipline.

The idea of disciplining a child feels unpleasant, but we know it's necessary to correct a child. It's likely that our emotions are tied to the action because we consistently think of discipline in its most negative form, as when we have to punish a child we love in order to halt an unacceptable behavior.

But discipline is much more than simply correcting poor behavior. Rather, the discipline we use with our children applies to the totality of their time under our care. Punishment for immoral actions is just one portion of it. We help our children become disciplined in their own minds and hearts by positively instructing them with the truths they need to live their lives. A biblical view of discipline allows parents to teach their children not only the consequences of sin but also the beauty of restoration.

This is why we can approach the idea of church discipline without a sour attitude. In fact, discipline is a positive and necessary action the church takes to help Christians grow up well in the faith.

Start

Welcome everyone to session 4 of *Basics*.

Use the following content to begin your time together.

When you hear the word *discipline,* maybe a negative image springs to mind. Our memories are flooded with images of a parent angrily correcting a child, a drill sergeant berating new soldiers, or the guilt associated with our inability to show self-control.

Perhaps because of these images, church discipline isn't a common occurrence. But it likely should be. But before we talk about how to practice it, we need to better understand what the Bible means by it.

> **If you've ever witnessed church discipline occur, describe how it happened and what its outcome was.**

Church discipline should come from the right motivation. Because the church has been entrusted with the gospel as its core doctrine, we must look to the way Jesus works in us to understand how discipline takes place in a congregation of believers.

In this session Pastor Juan Sanchez discusses church discipline and its importance in the local church. When it practices discipline correctly, the church is able to show the gospel to the world. Juan is the senior pastor of High Pointe Baptist Church in Austin, Texas.

Pray for God to open your hearts and minds before you watch the video for session 4.

Watch

Use the space below to follow along and take notes as you watch video session 4.

There are times in our lives when we will need to be corrected and put on the right path.

The life of a Christian is a life of discipline.

Church discipline is a mercy where they're experiencing a semblance of judgment, and they have an opportunity to repent and come back into the people of God.

The congregation has responsibility for church discipline.

The church is merely affirming their profession of faith: "You're not living according to the profession of faith that you made."

The process maintains the dignity of the person in sin.

We need to rearticulate the gospel. We need to rehearse the gospel. We need to practice the gospel.

There are going to be times when we falter and fail and we need one another, so the idea is not that we point out every single sin in every person's life.

Discuss

Use the following statements and questions to discuss the video.

We have various definitions of and ideas about the word *discipline*.

When you were a child, what was discipline like?

How does your experience with childhood discipline affect your thoughts about church discipline?

Pastor Juan Sanchez stated there are two types of discipline: formative and corrective. Each is necessary and rooted in God's redemptive work for us. Corrective discipline occurs in the larger context of formative discipline.

Read aloud Matthew 18:10-14.

Describe a time in your life when you were the lost sheep or when you witnessed the rescue of a lost sheep.

How does the context of love change the way we initiate church discipline?

We need to experience the mercy of corrective discipline so that we'll avoid God's necessary judgment of sin. In the story Jesus told, the lost sheep was in imminent danger. The shepherd's rescue work wasn't to scold the sheep but to deliver it back to the fold.

What's the ultimate purpose of church discipline?

Discipline doesn't happen from a hierarchical system of leadership. Rather, discipline is initiated by the congregation. When we read Matthew 18 and the instance of church discipline in 1 Corinthians 5 and 2 Corinthians 7, we see that the congregation collectively exercises corrective discipline with members who sin.

Read aloud Matthew 18:15-20.

Notice that Matthew 18:15-20 is preceded by the story of a shepherd who rescues one lost sheep and is followed by the parable of an unforgiving servant. How is your understanding of these verses affected by the surrounding passages?

The process Jesus outlined in Matthew 18:15-20 preserves the dignity of the people involved, especially the sinner. It offers a process of confrontation that begins with one believer going in private to another, thus offering friendship as a necessary part of corrective discipline. If the person continues to be unrepentant, however, the process must escalate until the circumstances are finally made public to the congregation.

Why are close relationships necessary for church discipline to accomplish its ultimate task of restoration?

How can a church create a culture of discipline that's rooted in the gospel?

Pray

As you reflect on the video teaching and the group discussion, you have an opportunity to pray for your church in specific ways. Here are some prayer priorities to focus on before the next group session.

- Unity in the life of your church as it encourages and admonishes one another in the gospel

- Faithfulness on the part of church members who are being tempted to stray from Christ

- Discernment by church leaders as they lead the church through difficult cases of discipline

- Receptive and repentant hearts by those who are under church discipline

- A holy witness in the church for the sake of its reputation among outsiders

- For unbelievers to turn to Jesus in repentance and faith

Prayer Requests

This Week's Plan

Worship

[ ] Read your Bible. Complete the reading plan on page 74.

[ ] Spend time with God by engaging with the devotional experience on page 75.

[ ] Spend time in daily prayer for the church and the members of the group.

Personal Study

[ ] Read and interact with "Discipline That Forms" on page 76.

[ ] Read and interact with "Discipline That Corrects" on page 80.

Application

[ ] Identify an area in your life where you need encouragement to be faithful in your walk with Jesus. Confide in a close Christian friend about this issue and ask him or her to pray with you.

[ ] Memorize Galatians 5:25: "Since we live by the Spirit, we must also follow the Spirit."

[ ] Add to your journal by recording ways your church is helping you walk in holiness. List ways your church leaders and members interact with you (preaching, fellowship, etc.) to encourage your maturity in Christ.

[ ] Pray for people who previously associated with your church but are now unfaithful to the Lord. Ask God how you should confront them about their sinful behavior.

Did you miss the group session?
Video sessions available for purchase at *lifeway.com/basics*

73

Read

Read the following Scripture passages this week. Use the acronym HEAR and the space provided to record your thoughts or action steps.

Day 1: Galatians 5:16-26

Day 2: Hebrews 12:3-11

Day 3: Matthew 16:24-28

Day 4: Matthew 18:10-20

Day 5: Matthew 18:21-35

Day 6: 1 Corinthians 5

Day 7: 2 Corinthians 2:5-11

Reflect

ACCOUNTABILITY

When Paul wrote his first letter to the Corinthian church, he had to address a touchy subject. In 1 Corinthians 5:1 he wrote:

> It is widely reported that there is sexual immorality among
> you, and the kind of sexual immorality that is not even tolerated
> among the Gentiles—a man is living with his father's wife.
> **1 Corinthians 5:1**

The message was clear that the church should remove the man from the active fellowship of believers. Paul's intent was for the man claiming Christ as his Lord to gain an acute awareness of his sin. Paul's second letter to that church indicates that the time had come for the man (if in fact he's referring to the same situation) to be restored. In 2 Corinthians 2:5-11 Paul urged restoration so that the man disciplined wouldn't become embittered against the church.

In the brief details we have of this incident, we see the arc of the story that should always accompany church discipline. It isn't a banner we wave to show how moral we are and how immoral "that person" is. Rather, it's an act done in the covenant relationship of the church to help a Christian understand the devastation that sin brings about in his or her life and possibly for eternity. Discipline is also used to preserve the reputation of the church and the perception of the gospel.

We often think of accountability as intrusive. It's quite the opposite in the body of Christ. God uses the church to call us closer to Himself and to the family of faith. Throughout our earthly lives our flesh will fail us. It will hunger for worldly pleasures, and our willpower is so feeble that it will give in. But under the guidance of the Word of God, the church can and should discipline and guide Christians to walk in a way that honors the Lord.

Personal Study 1

DISCIPLINE THAT FORMS

Discipline is an act the congregation takes to move people toward holiness. It's an action that both aids in forming our Christian character and calls us to account when we compromise our confession of faith in Christ. It's an action that keeps us aligned with what we profess to believe.

Understanding the Gospel

For discipline to fulfill its purpose of enabling believers to grow in our faith, we need to have a proper understanding of the gospel. Without the work of God through His good news, we can't hope to relate to Him or progress in our Christian maturity. What is the gospel?

The gospel is the good news that Jesus lived the perfect life that we should live; paid the penalty for sin in His death that we should pay; and rose from the dead, defeating sin and death. He now offers salvation to all who repent and believe, and He promises to come again and restore all things for those who are His.

> **How does having an accurate understanding of the gospel change the way you view church discipline?**

Understanding the gospel sets a proper foundation for church discipline. If we based discipline on something besides the gospel and the Scriptures, disaster would follow. First, we would become a church of Pharisees, where correction and instruction were used to prove our righteousness. Further, our goal for godliness would be replaced with the whim of what we thought was moral at that moment in time. Prioritizing God's Word and His plan for salvation will guide us to utilize church discipline for the purpose of helping believers grow in the likeness of Jesus.

Let's look at three different ways church discipline forms our character.

Discipline Serves as a Preventative Measure

We need to think clearly about the timing when we use church discipline.

> **Mark the time when you thought church discipline should be put into action before you began this study.**
> ☐ **From the beginning of the Christian walk**
> ☐ **At the time a Christian sins**
> ☐ **After a person has rejected the faith and the church**

Church discipline, when practiced correctly, begins at our salvation. This is evident from the meaning of the word *church*. The Greek word *ekklesia* literally means *called-out ones*. Christians are supposed to be different from people of the world. We're set aside or called out by God for a different purpose. To live as obedient children of God, we need accountability from the very beginning of our Christian lives.

As parents, we don't wait until our children reach their teenage years to train them in godly behavior. We begin as early as possible. We want to prevent the self-harm that comes from immoral behavior. We guide them toward their need of salvation and spiritual growth in Christ. Discipline in following the ways of God is the preventative measure that will guard them and shape their character.

> **Choose a sinful behavior below and describe how the church can exercise formative discipline to guide a believer to live out the faith.**

Adultery   Pride   Jealousy   Envy   Anger   Drunkenness

Discipline Instructs About Truth

In the Great Commission (see Matt. 28:18-20) Jesus said part of making disciples is "teaching them to observe everything I have commanded you" (v. 20).

> **List some of Jesus' commands in the Gospels that are sometimes difficult for you to follow.**

> **What actions could your church family take to help you keep these commands?**

The formative work of discipline is to lead people into the truth so that they won't be led into sin. God has given this responsibility to the church to guard the doctrine of the gospel and to proclaim it to the world. But we must not stop our instruction at the threshold of faith. Once people become Christians, they need to be instructed in the Christian life and doctrine.

> **In the following list of cultural issues and Christian doctrines, mark the ones you believe need more emphasis in your church. Plan a time when you can discuss them with a church leader.**
> ☐ Nature of marriage
> ☐ Hospitality
> ☐ Doctrine of salvation
> ☐ Doctrine of Scripture
> ☐ Doctrine of the Holy Spirit
> ☐ Doctrine of the church

Discipline Mentors and Models

When we become a Christian, we consent to the lordship of Christ in our lives. Simultaneously, God includes us in the church. By entering a congregation, we consent to live in covenant relationship with other believers. In these relationships we learn how to live out our Christian faith.

In Scripture we witness several examples of formative accountability in the New Testament church. In Acts 18:24-28 a powerful preacher named Apollos was incorrectly teaching about baptism. The married couple Priscilla and Aquila took him aside and explained to him the doctrine more fully. By doing so, they increased the effectiveness of his ministry. In the Book of 2 Timothy, the apostle Paul pointed out that the mother and the grandmother of the pastor Timothy had aided in Timothy's spiritual training (see v. 5). Family, friendship, and church membership all lead to the responsibility and privilege of serving as a model of disciplined faithfulness to the Lord.

How open are you to having a mentor in your life? Mark the scale.

✿———————————————————————————✿

Not ready   In some areas   Neutral   Need some help   Ready

Identify three people who've held you accountable for your past spiritual walk and list ways they've helped you in the faith.

The process of discipleship is paramount in the formative discipline of the church. In this work, truth is delivered in the fellowship of believers. Being mentored isn't about being lorded over by someone who's theologically smarter. Rather, it's participating in someone else's journey toward maturity.

We never know what God might be doing in a person's life or what plans He has for them. Therefore, no Christian should be left to struggle alone. Each person has an important role in God's kingdom and work. As we guide them through the discipline of discipleship, we equip them to more fully understand God's Word and to more faithfully walk in His ways.

Personal Study 2

DISCIPLINE THAT CORRECTS

The typical view of the word *discipline* has to do with correcting someone's behavior. Though church discipline begins with the formative work of discipleship and mentoring Christians in the faith, it includes corrective actions as well.

> Read Matthew 18:15-20. Why are the passages directly before and after important to Jesus' teaching on how to discipline a sinful person of faith?

Discipline Confronts Sinful Behavior

Church discipline is used to confront sin in the lives of believers. We don't use church discipline with unbelievers, because they aren't yet part of God's people. Instead, we confront them with the gospel's claims that they're condemned and in need of salvation. It's the loving action to take for someone who's perishing. Likewise, confronting Christians is the loving action to take when their sin is hampering their relationship with God and the church.

When we confront someone for their sinful behavior, our action must always be based on Scripture. Christ commissioned us to teach believers "to observe everything I have commanded you" (Matt. 28:20). Thus, there are zero commands of Jesus that are irrelevant or unworthy of obeying.

> Mark the following as helpful (*H*) or unhelpful (*U*) ways of confronting a Christian's sin.
> _____ Spontaneous confrontation in a Bible study
> _____ Private conversation
> _____ Ignoring the behavior and praying for them
> _____ Talking to your Bible-study group before approaching the person
> _____ Asking a pastor to deal with it
> _____ Talking to the person's spouse about the behavior
> _____ Confronting them through email or social media

Discipline Rebukes or Separates

The level or intensity of corrective discipline is often related to the person's response. Matthew 18:15 encourages us to begin the process by rebuking a brother in private. This action is to show a person his or her fault. It isn't a time for us to indulge in the sins of anger or malice. Rather, as those who recognize the forgiveness we've received from Christ, we should be humble and glad to help another find restoration.

Jesus' teachings in Matthew 18:16-20 guide our response if the rebuked Christian refuses to recognize his or her sin. The order presented respects privacy as long as it's helpful to the person being confronted.

> **What are the greatest reasons for the church's hesitation to personally confront people for their sin?**

After you've personally rebuked a person for sin, the next step is to take others with you for a second time of confrontation. Matthew 18:16 states that we take one or two others to serve as witnesses to the conversation.

> **Read Matthew 18:15-16. Record a few reasons that taking others with you is helpful to all parties involved.**

God gives the church as a whole the responsibility to direct doctrine and guide spiritual maturity. Taking others with you to rebuke an unrepentant Christian ensures that you aren't deceived or mistaken, prevents you from being tempted to sin, and provides witnesses to the hope of restoration. If the sinning Christian remains unrepentant, the church has one last recourse. The church is to be informed of the person's sin, and if the rebellious believer is still unrepentant, he or she must be treated as an unbeliever. Jesus described this step in Matthew 18:17, and He reiterated the authority of the church to take this step in verses 18-20.

Read Matthew 18:19-20. Why is God's presence so important to the work of corrective discipline?

These verses are often quoted to assure us that God will answer our prayers. But in fact, these verses have to do with the authority of the church to discipline and disciple believers. Verse 18 indicates that the church has both the authority and the responsibility to recognize who's a believer and who isn't. The church doesn't hold the power of salvation, but we deliver the message of Christ's salvation. In overseeing the membership of the church, we determine the status of those in our local church membership.

When Christians refuse to repent and refuse to heed the church's warnings, the church must choose to remove them from membership in the church. The purpose isn't to be harmful but to sound an alarm. When sinful Christians are disciplined this way, they no longer have access to the ministries that could care for their needs. This separation from Christian fellowship signals their separation from active fellowship with Christ due to their sin.

As we've seen, the purpose isn't to permanently separate people from the church. Our hope is that they'll come to their senses and seek restoration with the Lord.

Discipline Encourages Godly Sorrow

The work of church discipline is successful when godly sorrow takes hold of the rebellious heart. Paul wrote to the Corinthian church:

> I rejoice, not because you were grieved, but because your grief led to repentance. For you were grieved as God willed, so that you didn't experience any loss from us. For godly grief produces a repentance not to be regretted and leading to salvation, but worldly grief produces death. For consider how much diligence this very thing—this grieving as God wills—has produced in you: what a desire to clear yourselves, what indignation, what fear, what deep longing, what zeal, what justice! In every way you showed yourselves to be pure in this matter.
> **2 Corinthians 7:9-11**

Underline the phrases in this passage that describe the results of godly sorrow.

Worldly sorrow merely leads people to be sorry they were caught in sin. The attitude isn't one of repentance (or changing course) because of unrighteous behavior. Rather, they simply want to avoid any future embarrassment while continuing to live as they wish. They may promise to change but rarely fulfill the promise because worldly sorrow includes no heart transformation.

Paul stated it even more strongly in his words to the Corinthians: "Worldly grief produces death" (v. 10). Any repentance that doesn't lead people to their need for Christ's grace and mercy simply keeps them on a path of destruction.

As the church, we're afforded a great opportunity. We can lead people to the life-giving power of godly grief that's infused with repentance. As people turn their hearts toward the gospel message, they embrace the grace that gives life.

You likely know a fellow Christian who's struggling with sin. If so, list ways you'll take the first two steps of corrective discipline for this person.

An opening question I'll ask them in order to talk about this sin:

If necessary, the one or two persons I'll take with me for a second confrontation:

If necessary, the pastor I'll inform so that the church can take corrective action:

Record a prayer that God will soften this person's heart and will prepare him or her for repentance.

Church Leadership

Questions about church leadership often center on who does it rather than what it is.

In the church the ultimate authority is held by Jesus as our Chief Shepherd and Head of the church. But the Lord has also given authority to the church to guide people toward the message of salvation and to disciple one another. To facilitate the church's ministry, the New Testament provides the qualifications and duties of church leaders.

Sometimes having a person in authority over us isn't perceived as positive. In our culture clawing our way to the top of the corporate structure is applauded, and being the master of our own fate is rewarded. But as believers, we must welcome and learn from godly leadership that holds authority and guides us. With elder-led congregationalism the whole congregation possesses authority, but the Holy Spirit calls some to serve as pastors or elders whose work is to lead the church in using its authority.

Godly leadership is one of God's great gifts to the church. Through it we see a picture of Jesus. By it we act with the authority God has granted the church to display the gospel and to proclaim it to the world. Let's take a look at church leadership and learn the privilege it holds to guide God's people.

Start

Welcome everyone to session 5 of *Basics*.

Use the following content to begin your time together.

Leadership is everywhere. We witness it at work, at home, and in virtually every arena of life. It's been defined with complex academic essays and simple, quotable sentences about influencing those around you.

What are some primary characteristics of the leaders in your church?

In this session we'll discuss the church-leadership roles that are identified in the New Testament. God knew the church would need leaders for many different reasons. Because Jesus isn't physically present, we need spiritually mature leaders who can teach us God's Word and care for the congregation.

How is leadership in a church different from leadership in other organizations?

Leadership is both a gift and a responsibility. As we understand more about the foundations of the church, we can see that having leaders is a blessing. The Bible teaches us to gladly follow the people God places in positions of leadership.

Let's see what Pastor Mark Dever has to say about the roles of leadership in the church and how they can guide the church in its kingdom work. Mark is the senior pastor of Capitol Hill Baptist Church in Washington, D.C.

Pray for God to open your hearts and minds before you watch the video for session 5.

Watch

Use the space below to follow along and take notes as you watch video session 5.

Three Functions of Deacons

1. To care for the physical needs of the church
2. To help the unity of the church
3. To support the ministry of the Word being done by the elders

How to Relate to Church Leaders

1. Be thankful.
2. Pray for them.
3. Pay for them.
4. Gossip about them positively.
5. Sow seeds of appreciation.

All the pastors in your church should feel a tender regard for, a love, an esteem for all of the sheep and especially the weaker or more awkward ones.

How to Pray for Your Leaders

1. The passages that are going to be preached on
2. The encouragement of the pastor's family
3. The pastor's health
4. The pastor's understanding of the Word
5. The pastor's wisdom and discernment
6. The things Paul prayed for the churches at the beginning of his epistles

Aspiring to Become a Church Leader

1. Be a good member.
2. Don't wait till somebody tells you that you can function as a teacher of God's Word.

Discuss

Use the following statements and questions to discuss the video.

Pastor Mark Dever stated that there are two roles of leadership in the church: elders and deacons. He explained that the words *elder, overseer, shepherd,* and *pastor* are used interchangeably in the New Testament.

Describe the difference between the two roles of elder and deacon.

Read aloud Timothy 3:1-7.

What are some major characteristics we should look for in potential elders?

God raises up elders from the congregation to give direction to the members. These leaders provide direction by understanding and teaching the Scriptures. Not all teaching comes in the form of a preaching ministry in worship services. Some comes in the elder's ministry as a Bible-study leader, in discipling relationships, or in providing scriptural guidance for the church's ministry.

What type of attitude should elders have toward a congregation?

Leaders in the church should feel the weighty responsibility of leadership, but it should never drive them to prideful behavior. People who teach the Word have the great privilege of aiding fellow Christians in their spiritual maturity. But this leadership isn't a license to become dictatorial or demanding. Instead, leaders need to have a posture of humble service.

Read aloud 1 Timothy 3:8-13.

What are some major characteristics we should look for in potential deacons?

What does the word *likewise* in verse 8 signal to us?

Deacons serve in a caring, supporting role for the church. By their work to ensure that needs are met, they help preserve a congregation's unity. The neglect of church members' needs is a sad commentary about the church. Bitterness is often the result. But when people are cared for, a bold picture of the gospel is presented to the community.

Read aloud Acts 6:1-7.

What were the responsibilities of the first men who served in deaconlike ministry?

Because of their faithfulness what was the result in the church?

The preaching and teaching of God's Word are central to the life of the church. Without the proclamation of the true gospel, the church will fall into disarray and lose its distinctiveness in the world.

How do the roles of elders and deacons aid in keeping God's Word as a priority in the church?

Describe the way members of the congregation should relate to and feel about their leaders.

Pray

As you reflect on the video teaching and the group discussion, you have an opportunity to pray for your church in specific ways. Here are some prayer priorities to focus on before the next group session.

- Unity in the church's leadership and unified support of the leaders by the congregation as a whole

- Faithfulness by pastors and elders in their work of leadership

- For church leaders to discern God's direction for the church

- Compassionate hearts for those who serve as deacons

- For members of the congregation to have evangelistic passion

- For unbelievers to turn to Jesus in repentance and faith

Prayer Requests

This Week's Plan

Worship

[ ] Read your Bible. Complete the reading plan on page 92.

[ ] Spend time with God by engaging with the devotional experience on page 93.

[ ] Spend time in daily prayer for the church and the members of the group.

Personal Study

[ ] Read and interact with "Deacons: Leadership Through Service" on page 94.

[ ] Read and interact with "Elders and Pastors: Service Through Leadership" on page 98.

Application

[ ] Memorize Hebrews 13:7: "Remember your leaders who have spoken God's word to you. As you carefully observe the outcome of their lives, imitate their faith."

[ ] Use your journal to write a prayer for the leaders in your church. Ask God to give them discernment about the work of the church, insight into His Word, and courage to lead in His mission.

[ ] Seek out a leader in the church who needs encouragement. Ask for a time to meet without any personal agenda of meeting your own needs. Instead, find ways you can build up his faith.

[ ] Work alongside your church leaders to seek unity in the church. If an issue is causing disruption, ask the leaders how you can assist them.

Did you miss the group session?
Video sessions available for purchase at *lifeway.com/basics*

91

Read

Read the following Scripture passages this week. Use the acronym HEAR and the space provided to record your thoughts or action steps.

Day 1: Acts 6:1-7

Day 2: 1 Timothy 3:1-7

Day 3: 1 Timothy 3:8-13

Day 4: Luke 12:35-48

Day 5: Acts 20:17-38

Day 6: Titus 1:5-9

Day 7: Hebrews 13:7-19

Reflect

TRUE LEADERSHIP

Leadership is a great gift from God. But who has it? The ultimate authority for the church lies with Christ, its Head. Christians, living as the community of faith, are the body of Christ, and He directs us in all our ways. We follow Him in the collective ministries of the church and in the personal outworking of our faith.

Yet God has graciously provided authority to the church to establish and practice leadership. That leadership isn't given to the governments of nations, ivory-tower intellectuals, or pious clergymen who are hidden away from the sight of the world. Instead, God has given the authority of leadership to the congregation as a whole. Congregational church government allows each local body of believers to find direction from the Word of God through the Holy Spirit's guidance. The local body of believers then leads itself under the sovereignty of Christ, working through the congregation's authority and the leaders it appoints.

We set leaders apart from the rest of the congregation because we need their training and guidance in gospel ministry. We should be consistently grateful for our church leaders. Hebrews 13:17 reminds us to obey the leaders of the church because "they keep watch over your souls as those who will give an account."

As the church, we must operate under the direction of church leaders but never try to usurp the eternal reign of Christ over the church. When the leaders do their work by recognizing the borrowed nature of their authority, they can do so with gladness. As members of the church, we also accept their leadership with gladness, knowing they're acting as living portraits of Christ's work in our lives.

Personal Study 1

DEACONS: LEADERSHIP THROUGH SERVICE

The theme of service is a prominent one throughout the Bible. In the Old Testament the judges appointed by God served by settling disputes and leading people toward repentance. The Old Testament prophets served by delivering God's message to humanity. The New Testament records the ultimate act of service in Jesus' death and resurrection. When the church was born, it expressed service as an outflow of the gospel's work in Christians.

Service is specifically tied in the church to the office of the deacon. The Greek word often translated as *deacon* is *diakonos*. In its most literal form it means *servant*. However, to better understand the office it designates, we transliterate the word as *deacon*. (*Transliterate* means *to write the word with the closest associated letters in our own language*.)

> **What have you normally perceived to be the work of deacons in your church?**
> ☐ **Making strategic decisions**
> ☐ **Serving the needs of widows and orphans**
> ☐ **Providing spiritual guidance for people in trouble**
> ☐ **Calling wayward Christians to repent**
> ☐ **Distributing the elements of the Lord's Supper**
> ☐ **Leading prayer in church gatherings**
> ☐ **Other:**

Who Is a Deacon?

It's generally accepted that the deacon ministry was launched through the episode we read about in Acts 6:1-7 Though the office of deacon isn't named in this passage, the verbal form *to deacon* is used in verse 2: "to serve tables." From this passage we can easily see the prototype for the work of deacons in the church.

Read Acts 6:1-7. Describe the work deacons were called to do.

What effect did the work of deacons have on the work done
by the apostles and by the other leaders of the church?

The role of deacon isn't for just anyone who wishes to serve. The qualifications for the position are given in both Acts 6:1-7 and I Timothy 3:8-13.
Deacons are to be "full of the Spirit and wisdom" (Acts 6:3). Whereas
many people can do the physical work of ministry, the early church first
appointed those who were spiritually mature.

What difference does it make that deacons are to be spiritually
mature rather than just willing people who want to serve?

Later in I Timothy 3:8-13 the apostle Paul outlined the character traits
necessary for a deacon to possess. The qualifications range from exercising
self-control to being a strong leader in the home. By giving moral and
character qualifications for a deacon, Paul emphasized that ministry on
behalf of the church isn't a practical matter but a spiritual one. A deacon's
work displays the core message of the church. Deacons don't just do a job.
They minister through the power of the gospel to display the effects of the
gospel when a life is transformed by the gospel.

Now let's look at three major categories of work done by deacons. Again,
we'll look to Acts 6:1-7 for help in understanding the work of deacons.

Care for the Physical Needs of the Church

As the apostles went about their work in the early church, they were being saddled with the need "to handle financial matters" (Acts 6:1). Different translations of the Bible use different phrases for this work:

- "To handle financial matters" (HCSB)
- "To wait on tables" (NIV)
- "To serve tables" (ESV, NASB, NKJV)
- "To look after the accounts" (Phillips)
- "Running a food program" (NLT)

The context of verse 1 helps us understand the work that needed to be accomplished. The Greek widows were being neglected by the church, and the church body needed to collect and distribute resources (financial and otherwise) to care for the needy. So the apostles led the church to appoint people who could assume responsibility for this work. It's easy to understand why people appointed to distribute money and food needed to have upstanding spiritual character.

The work of deacons isn't necessarily glamorous. Meeting physical needs can be relationally challenging. But this work must be done in order for the church to accomplish its ministry to one another.

> **List physical needs in your church congregation that the deacons can have a role in meeting.**

Work for Unity in the Body

Deacons minister in order to meet physical needs. But they also do the work in such a way that it accomplishes important spiritual work for the whole church. By meeting needs fairly, deacons protect the unity of the church.

In Acts 6 those who were being neglected were the widows of Greek descent. Meanwhile, the Jewish widows were provided for sufficiently. The ministry met physical needs and put a halt to a potential rift in the congregation.

What are the most likely issues to cause division in your church?

How can the deacons work in a way that will resolve those issues?

Deacons are able "to bind the church together with cords of kindness and loving service."[1]

Support the Ministry of the Word

It's clear from the apostles' words in Acts 6:2-4 that the ministry to the widows needed to be done by someone other than the apostles. As we read all throughout the New Testament, the church is a body made up of many parts, with each member fulfilling its own God-assigned role. First Corinthians 12:18 states, "God has placed each one of the parts in one body just as He wanted." The apostles' role was to fulfill the ministry of the Word and prayer. They didn't want the widows or anyone else to be neglected, but neither did they want to neglect the responsibilities to which God had called them.

The answer was simple then, and it's still simple today. The ministry of the deacons is to serve needs, thus freeing elders and pastors to guide the church through the Scriptures. As deacons do their work, elders and pastors can do their work. They aren't in competition for attention but support one another in gospel-focused ministries.

Compose a prayer for the deacons in your church. Thank God for their ministry and pray that they'll have joy in their work.

1. Jonathan Leeman and Mark Dever, *Understanding Church Leadership* (Nashville: B&H Publishing Group, 2016), 14.

Personal Study 2

ELDERS & PASTORS: SERVICE THROUGH LEADERSHIP

What does it take to be a good leader? Depending on where you look, the results will vary to a wide degree. When you look in Scripture, however, you find a consistent answer. Leadership in the church is to function in such a way that the congregation strengthens its allegiance to Christ. This is likely why the New Testament usually addresses the office of elder or pastor in a plural form (see Acts 14:23; 16:4; 20:17; 21:18; I Tim. 4:14; Titus 1:5; Jas. 5:14; and I Pet. 5:1).

How does a plurality of elders help keep a church's focus on Christ?

What happens in a church when one person is allowed to make all the decisions and hold the authority of the church single-handedly?

The terms *elder, overseer,* and *pastor* are used interchangeably in the Bible. The fact that these words are most often used in a plural form illustrates that church leadership grows from the congregation's authority. The congregation doesn't invest its gospel authority in one man who tries to be a superhero who meets all the congregation's needs. Instead, by having a plurality of elders, the congregation maintains authority as a whole rather than fighting one man who becomes tempted to supplant the Lord's authority. Let's look into the specific work of elders.

Preach and Teach

When Paul wrote to Timothy about the basic qualifications of elders, he included the ability to teach (see I Tim. 3:2). Because the church has one authoritative source of truth in the Bible, elders should be prepared and equipped to teach the Word to the church. In response the church must be prepared to gladly receive biblical teaching from the elders.

Preaching and teaching are primary forms of leadership in the church. Distinguishing between the two will help us gain a more complete view of an elder's leadership.

Preaching is often associated with a vocational member of the church staff, though not always. Preaching occurs in public meetings such as worship services and evangelistic meetings. Not all elders hold an office for which they need to preach, but all elders should be spiritually equipped to teach in other environments. An elder is to be prepared to make disciples through God's Word in one-on-one relationships and in small-group Bible studies. The ability and willingness to teach ensures that the elder points people to the source of truth instead of guiding them to rely on humans for hope and even salvation. As gospel-centered leaders, elders focus people on Christ.

Pray

When deacons were set apart to care for widows in Acts 6:1-7, the purpose was so that the apostles (the elders of the church) could devote their time to the Word and to prayer. Prayer was so important that the early leaders of the church made it one of their primary responsibilities. Too often our church leaders give in to the same temptation they preach and teach against: making prayer the last resort rather than the first option.

Elders set priorities for the congregation as they lead by their example. Placing prayer as a priority for themselves and for church gatherings will lead Christians to do the same in their personal relationships with Christ.

As elders lead in lifting up the importance of prayer, they demonstrate that they and the whole church are dependent on the Lord. Everyone needs God for salvation, sanctification, and every provision in life.

Shepherd

Elders do the work of shepherding the congregation. Preaching and teaching require preparation. Prayer requires perseverance. Shepherding requires initiative. The overseers of the church should be spiritually mature so that they can intervene to meet needs before lives spin out of control.

The ancient image of a shepherd is one of hard work and careful attention. A good shepherd knows the needs of the individual sheep and has the skill to meet those needs. This work requires love and patience.

Shepherding also requires humility. Both oversight and pastoral care are done with the realization that church members don't belong to the elders. Rather, elders are undershepherds to the Great Shepherd, Jesus. But that humility brings great joy and even greater comfort. Because the members of the church are the Lord's, He has provided, is providing, and will provide for their needs. As shepherds, elders can rely on the Holy Spirit's empowering work to skillfully carry out pastoral ministry.

What needs do you have for which you need pastoral care?

How can one of the elders or pastors in your church assist you in your struggles?

Holding its authority under Christ, the congregation should consistently encourage the pastors or elders to initiate shepherding work. It's foolhardy to have men in these biblical positions and then refuse them access to our lives. God has given them as a gift to the church and holds them accountable for this work. They're glad to do it, and we should gladly receive their aid.

Describe the weekly work done by the pastor(s) in your church.

Oversee

Paul admonished the elders of the church in Ephesus as he was preparing to depart:

> Be on guard for ourselves and for all the flock that the Holy
> Spirit has appointed you to as overseers, to shepherd the
> church of God, which He purchased with His own blood.
> **Acts 20:28**

Paul's statement was a challenge to the leaders and a warning about the serious nature of oversight for the church. Elders must be careful not to simply adopt the model of corporate manager for the congregation. Their work is more than administrating decisions about church programming and calendaring.

Read Acts 20:26-31 and summarize the work of an elder's oversight in light of these verses.

Elders are tasked with guarding the church's membership and doctrine. They act as warriors for the faith to defend biblical beliefs and to protect the church from error. They also speak on behalf of the church about membership. Though they don't have the power to save a person, elders serve as the voice of the church about the status of a person's faithfulness to the gospel and the evidence of saving transformation.

Elders have before them a wonderful but difficult task. As church members, we have a responsibility to follow them, pray for them, and encourage them in their gospel-centered work.

The Great Commission

The Great Commission. Just the sound of that phrase sounds important.

When Jesus left the earth to ascend back to the Father, He commanded His followers not to remain alone in their faith but to go and make disciples. Rather than huddle up and allow the message of salvation to die with them, they were commissioned to spread this good news around the globe.

This commission to spread the gospel has a definite end in mind: more disciples of Jesus. It's one of the primary purposes for which the church exists. All His followers are to spread the fame of Jesus as widely as possible so that people can hear the good news of salvation and respond to Him in faith.

We specifically refer to Jesus' words in Matthew 28:18-20 as the Great Commission. However, several statements Jesus made at other places in the Gospels express the same imperative. As we explore this great mission from God, we'll see that it's one more way He works in the church to develop believers and magnify His name for His glory.

Start

Welcome everyone to session 6 of *Basics*.

Use the following content to begin your time together.

The nature of the church and the commission of the church go hand in hand. It's through understanding the *why* of the church that we can then understand the *what* and *how* of our ministry together as the body of Christ.

> **What would you describe as the mission, vision, or strategy of your local congregation? If your church has a mission or vision statement, discuss the way it guides the work of your church.**

Jesus clearly laid out His plan for the church before He ascended back to heaven. It's evident from the way Jesus taught His disciples that multiplying the number of followers on the earth was unmistakably Jesus' intention for the church. This mission isn't something individual believers can accomplish on their own. Jesus gave this task to us as local congregations of believers.

In this session Pastor Robby Gallaty lays out a compelling argument that disciple making is the centerpiece of the life of a local church. From Jesus' teachings to the mission work we see throughout the New Testament, the church is designed to deepen the walks of Christians and to persuade more people to become followers of Jesus.

As you move through this final session, consider how all the foundational tasks of the church work together to accomplish Jesus' Great Commission. Robby is the senior pastor of Long Hollow Baptist Church in Hendersonville, Tennessee.

Pray for God to open your hearts and minds before you watch the video for session 6.

Watch

Use the space below to follow along and take notes as you watch video session 6.

The Great Commission always happens in the local church.

Two Parts of the Great Commission

1. Inviting people to a relationship with Jesus
2. Investing—walking with people through the journey of life

Two Commands in the Great Commission

1. "Go therefore and make disciples" (v. 19, ESV).
2. "Behold, I am with you always (v. 20, ESV).

Jesus said go make disciples, not converts. There's a big difference.

Discipleship is not a class you take. It's the course of one's life.

As people focus on the depth of their walk with Christ, God begins to take care of the breadth of their ministry.

People underestimate what they can do, empowered by the Spirit of God, wielding the Word of God.

When people really get that God's called them to be involved in making disciples, they take ownership of their faith.

In the kindness of God, He wants us to participate in His Great Commission and in the great adventure.

Discuss

Use the following statements and questions to discuss the video.

Jesus gave the Great Commission to the church. He wasn't speaking to a certain individual who was then to pass it along one by one through the world. Rather, Jesus gave His commission to all the disciples.

Read aloud Matthew 28:16-20.

How does the promise of Jesus' presence with the disciples change the way we go about fulfilling the Great Commission?

When you feel fearful, nervous, or anxious about sharing the gospel with another person, how will these verses change your attitude?

What part of the Great Commission is your church doing very well? What part needs more attention?

There's a difference between making converts and making disciples. Pastor Robby Gallaty emphasized that as churches deepen the walks of disciples, God takes care of increasing the number of disciples. An attitude of faith in God's continued care and involvement helps us respond positively to His commission to make disciples.

What's the difference between the way a convert lives and the way a disciple lives?

How would you like to refine the scorecard in the church to better reflect Jesus' priorities in the Great Commission?

The apostle Paul was determined to see the church grow during his lifetime. He had been saved from a life of murderous sin that opposed the church. Through his three missionary trips he worked to evangelize Jews, share the gospel with Gentiles, and plant churches. He devoted his life to making disciples. One man he trained to serve as a pastor/elder of a church was Timothy. Paul's two letters to Timothy gave instructions about building up the church.

Read aloud 2 Timothy 2:2.

Describe the way Timothy was to pass along the truth of God's Word.

What does Paul's instruction to Timothy teach us about carrying out the Great Commission?

God is pleased with us because we're Christ's disciples. On the basis of Christ's death and resurrection, the Father has declared us righteous in His sight. Now, like the first-century disciples, we must move forward in the mission to make disciples with God's presence and power. As they went out to spread the gospel and returned from their ministry, Jesus had a distinctive response to their ministry.

Read aloud Luke 10:17-21.

Consider the idea that Jesus was overjoyed by the work of the disciples. What work of your local church gives Jesus joy?

Pray

As you reflect on the video teaching and the group discussion, you have an opportunity to pray for your church in specific ways. Here are some prayer priorities to focus on before the next group session.

- Unity in the life of your church to a degree that gives credibility to your public witness

- A growing culture of disciple making among church members, so that working together to evangelize increasingly becomes an ordinary part of the church's life

- That your church leaders would grow in their personal evangelism and disciple making and that their example would spread

- A growing compassion for and empathy toward lost friends and neighbors among members of the church

- Growth in the fear of God among members, leading to more courage to evangelize

- For unbelievers to turn to Jesus in repentance and faith

Prayer Requests

This Week's Plan

Worship

[ ] Read your Bible. Complete the reading plan on page 110.

[ ] Spend time with God by engaging with the devotional experience on page 111.

[ ] Spend time in daily prayer for the church and the members of the group.

Personal Study

[ ] Read and interact with "Extending the Church" on page 112.

[ ] Read and interact with "Beyond Conversion" on page 116.

Application

[ ] Add to your journal by making a list of friends who need to hear the gospel. As you make this list, pray for these people individually and ask the Lord for opportunities to witness to them.

[ ] Memorize John 20:21: "Jesus said to them again, 'Peace to you! As the Father has sent Me, I also send you.' "

[ ] Take time to analyze any reasons you aren't making disciples. Identify things that make you nervous and anxious. Then lay the issues before God so that He can strengthen you for obedience to His mission.

[ ] Commit to continue your journey of growing as a disciple and as a healthy church member after this study.

Did you miss the group session?
Video sessions available for purchase at *lifeway.com/basics*

109

Read

Read the following Scripture passages this week. Use the acronym HEAR and the space provided to record your thoughts or action steps.

Day 1: Matthew 28:18-20

Day 2: John 20:19-23

Day 3: Acts 1:1-8

Day 4: Romans 1:13-23

Day 5: Mark 12:28-34

Day 6: Acts 11:19-26

Day 7: Revelation 7:9-17

Reflect

A PASSION FOR OTHERS

God created the world to reflect His glory. Of all His creation God chose to place His own image only in human beings. It's an amazing privilege to be created in the image of God.

We marred that image by our sin, but God had a plan for our redemption. He provided for Adam and Eve in spite of their disobedience. When humanity degenerated into a state of gross iniquity, God provided for the salvation of Noah and his family. He made Abraham and his descendants into the great nation of Israel. Through the Old Testament God gave the law, judges, prophets, and kings as a constant call for us to return to Him. He desired and still desires to fashion a people for His own.

Finally, Christ was sent to purchase our salvation. In His crucifixion God executed our spiritual death and restored Christians to a right relationship with Him. We enter the church and work alongside other believers to extend the great message of the gospel to the world. We want every image bearer of God to hear of the salvation He offers.

Having received salvation, you're now called to freely share this gift with others. God desires to work through you and your local church to extend His redemptive grace throughout the world.

Personal Study 1

EXTENDING THE CHURCH

The Great Commission is a phrase we use to refer to Jesus' command to His followers at the end of the Gospel of Matthew. It comes after the great redemptive work of Jesus' death and resurrection.

> **As you read the following passage, underline the words or phrases that indicate the disciples' response to Jesus. Circle the words or phrases that are Jesus' commands to His disciples.**

> The 11 disciples traveled to Galilee, to the mountain where Jesus had directed them. When they saw Him, they worshiped, but some doubted. Then Jesus came near and said to them, "All authority has been given to Me in heaven and on earth. Go, therefore, and make disciples of all nations, baptizing them in the name of the Father and of the Son and of the Holy Spirit, teaching them to observe everything I have commanded you. And remember, I am with you always, to the end of the age."
> **Matthew 28:16-20**

Jesus didn't give this command to an individual member of His group of followers. Rather, He spoke it to all His disciples. As we trace the various commission passages throughout Jesus' ministry and the New Testament, we find that there's a collective responsibility to accomplish God's mission. Let's take a look at some features of this call.

The Bookends

To fully embrace Jesus' commission requires us to come fully under God's sovereign will. The church is never left to do the work of God without the power of God. Jesus told His followers in verse 18, "All authority has been given to Me." Then in verse 20 He stated, "I am with you always, to the end of the age." These two statements form bookends for Jesus' commission.

What difference does it make that Jesus claims all authority and then promises His presence to believers?

List some reasons it matters to the church as a whole that Christ's authoritative presence accompanies a local congregation as it obeys God's mission.

If Jesus left us only these instructions about what to do as a church, we could be grateful. How much more should we praise Him for giving us a commission and guaranteeing to be with us as we complete it?

The Great Commission bookends of Jesus' power and Jesus' presence give us assurance we can't gain any other way. The church can operate in Jesus' authority to proclaim the gospel. It also works in faith, knowing God won't be thwarted in carrying out His will.

The Commission

The central phrase we most often focus on in the Great Commission is "Go ... and make disciples" (v. 19). In the original language the form of the verb *go* conveys continual action. Therefore, Jesus' command wasn't to identify a particular place and go there to make disciples. Rather, making disciples is work we do *as we're going* in all circumstances and places in life.

Make a list of different places you spend your time each day. On a scale of 1 (low) to 5 (high), rate how well you're sharing the gospel in those places. For example, "Work: 3."

As believers, we share the faith individually as part of our church work. It's what church members do. We go into the world to explain the gospel and call people to follow Jesus. It's important to note that Jesus didn't ask for us to recruit nominal converts, schedule people to be religiously busy, or ask people to simply modify their moral code. Rather, we're to "make disciples" (v. 19).

Of All Nations

The context in which the church is to make disciples of Jesus is "all nations" (v. 19). Jesus gave to the church a global mandate. Consider the companion commission Jesus gave in Acts 1:8:

> You will receive power when the Holy Spirit has come
> on you, and you will be My witnesses in Jerusalem,
> in all Judea and Samaria, and to the ends of the earth.
> **Acts 1:8**

The church isn't intended to be localized to one set of people. In Jesus' command in Matthew 28, the word used for *nations* in verse 19 means *people group*. When this idea is coupled with the Acts 1:8 commission, it's clear that God intends for the church to carry the gospel to all the peoples of the world. In the Old Testament Israel served as a sign of God's reign over the earth. The Old Testament covenant was given through Abraham and expressed through the law. Israel's job was to live out the covenant. This included inviting the nations of the world to worship the one true God.

As the church under the new covenant of salvation through Jesus, we carry God's mission forward by making disciples of Jesus. The actions of the first-century church, recorded from Acts through Revelation, delivered the gospel to both Jews and Gentiles. The church spread throughout the Roman Empire and beyond.

List at least five places in your city, state, nation, or world that
you know need a stronger gospel witness.

Sometimes our preferences and sin get in the way of our fulfilling Jesus'
commission. In the opening chapters of Acts, the church was led by and
primarily made up of members who were of Jewish descent. In that culture
Jews didn't generally associate with Gentiles (everyone who wasn't Jewish),
a principle that was especially true in regard to religious affiliation.

In Acts 10:1-8 an angel visited a Gentile named Cornelius and told him
to send messengers to Joppa to find a man named Simon Peter.

Read the rest of the story in Acts 10:9-48. Then write a summary
of the story. Who are the main characters? What did God ask them
to do? What was their response? How did it change the view of the
church toward its mission?

Racism, favoritism, and other forms of discrimination all run counter to
the commission God has given to the church. Instead, we're to operate
with our gospel-oriented authority and proclaim the message of Christ.
Church leaders like Peter share the gospel in both private settings and
public forums. Throughout the Book of Acts, Paul confronted sinners with
the gospel, challenged politicians with the claims of Jesus' sovereignty, and
delivered to all people the truth that Jesus is the Messiah.

The Great Commission calls the church to carry the whole message of our
sin and God's salvation to the whole world. It's the only truth that can bring
men and women from every tongue, tribe, and nation into a right relationship
with God.

Personal Study 2

BEYOND CONVERSION

When people become disciples of Jesus, they're just beginning. As you've already studied, Christians become members of the church. In a local congregation believers learn to work in the authority of a congregation; follow those in biblically defined leadership positions; and act according to biblical practices such as discipline, financial stewardship, and the ordinances.

From Commission to Commitment

One of the ordinances, you'll remember, is baptism. In the Great Commission given by Jesus, He commanded the church to baptize people who become disciples (see Matt. 28:19). Throughout the New Testament and church history, we witness that practice.

> **Read Acts 8:26-40. The Ethiopian man wanted to be baptized in response to the gospel Philip shared with him. Why was it a radical event for this man to be baptized? What do you think his baptism signaled to all the people in his caravan?**

Because the church is the entity that normally administers baptism, it's important to keep this ordinance closely tied to our commission from Jesus. As we've studied, baptism is more than a religious ritual. It represents the fact that a person has confessed Christ is Lord, and it acknowledges his or her entry into the church. As the church baptizes, it gives a public sign that the person has truly repented and placed his or her faith in Christ for salvation.

> **Describe the most recent baptism observed by your church. What life change was represented by this person's baptism?**

Teaching Everything

The next part of the Great Commission is perhaps the most overlooked. Yet when the church places proper emphasis on it, the results will be meaningful membership and commitment to God's Word. Jesus' command included "teaching them to observe everything I have commanded you" (Matt. 28:20).

When Jesus stated that we're to teach disciples how to obey all His commands, He meant all His commands. We aren't allowed to pick and choose what we think is important and what isn't.

We already know how teaching all Jesus' commands can occur in a local congregation. The church has authority to declare who's a member and who isn't. The Bible identifies positions of leadership and service for instructing disciples in the Word. The church—both leaders and members—hold one another accountable through church discipline so that the process of discipleship infuses our lives.

> **For each of these categories, give one example of how instruction in Jesus' commands can take place or has taken place in your life.**
>
> **The church identifies a new Christian:**
>
> **Elders or pastors equip Christians:**
>
> **Members mentor others in the faith:**

In the midst of his letter to the Ephesian Christians, Paul reminded them that they should be unified in their work, even though there was a diversity of gifts among them. The work the Holy Spirit was doing in them wasn't for the sake of pride but for humble service for one another's maturity. All members of a local congregation must teach one another as part of its work to equip one another to live in the power of the gospel. Paul wrote:

Since you put away lying, speak the truth, each one to
his neighbor, because we are members of one another.
Ephesians 4:25

No foul language is to come from your mouth, but only what is good for
building up someone in need, so that it gives grace to those who hear.
Ephesians 4:29

How can your Bible-study group actively guard one another from the sins warned about in these verses?

How can you actively encourage character development among members of your group outside the times you meet together?

The work we must do for one another is most comfortably the work of
positive encouragement. But as you see from the verses in Ephesians, we must
warn as well. As members of one body, we have the responsibility to keep
one another away from sin. But we don't do so by bludgeoning one another
with guilt. The apostle Paul taught that we disciple one another to focus
on the truth of the gospel so that sin becomes too burdensome to enjoy:

I am amazed that you are so quickly turning away from Him who called you
by the grace of Christ and are turning to a different gospel—not that there
is another gospel, but there are some who are troubling you and want to
change the good news about the Messiah. But even if we or an angel from
heaven should preach to you a gospel other than what we have preached to
you, a curse be on him! As we have said before, I now say again: If anyone
preaches to you a gospel contrary to what you received, a curse be on him!
Galatians 1:6-9

What are some false gospels you hear today?

In what ways is the true gospel superior to these false teachings?

Planting Churches

Paul and the other leaders of the church in the New Testament established new churches. A commitment to God's mission should encourage personal evangelism and personal involvement in discipleship throughout the membership of a church. Actions done on a personal level should always be coupled with what's done on a shared level as a church body. Making disciples, baptizing them, and teaching them Christ's commands should result in a desire to multiply both the number of disciples and the number of congregations that make disciples.

When Jesus sent us into the world to carry out His mission, this sending was for the church as a whole. The mission of God is to multiply the number of believers by multiplying the number of churches. And vice versa. These two impulses within God's commission go hand in hand, never in competition. One always facilitates the other.

How can your church more effectively—
give toward the work of church planting?

pray for church plants in your community?

aid church plants in other countries?

Have you ever prayed about the possibility of participating in a church plant in order to support a new work? In what ways can you be personally involved in church planting?

Leader Guide

Opening and Closing Group Sessions

Always try to engage each person at the beginning of a group session. Once a person speaks, even if only to answer a generic question, he or she is more likely to speak up later about more personal matters.

You may want to begin each session by reviewing the previous week's personal study. This review provides context for the new session and opportunities to share relevant experiences, application, or truths learned between sessions. Then set up the theme of the study to prepare personal expectations.

Always open and close the session with prayer, recognizing that only the Holy Spirit provides understanding and transformation in our lives. (The prayer suggestions provided in each session help focus members on Scripture, key truths, and personal application from the week's teaching.)

Remember that your goal isn't just meaningful discussion but discipleship.

Session 1: Congregational Authority

Summary statements help clarify key teaching points and provide direction for the questions that follow. (You'll do this several times in each session.)

Always keep God's Word central in group discussions. Ultimately, you want to hear what God says. Asking someone to read Scripture can engage more people in the topic of study.

Describe the way your congregation works together for God's glory.

What's the job of a congregation?

A key question we must ask about the work of the church is "Who leads in these practices?" How would you answer this question?

How should the church choose the people who hold offices?

Questions about who will serve in roles in the church can spark conversations about who currently holds those places. Carefully guide the discussion so that it doesn't become a complaint session about the work done by current leaders.

What would cause a congregation to want their ears tickled rather than to hear the truth of Scripture?

This is a question that will challenge group members to face their own roles in the church. Such questions are designed to challenge previous thinking.

When the truth isn't taught by the church, who bears the weight of responsibility—the leaders or the congregation? Explain.

How does congregational authority facilitate evangelism?

What's the congregation's role in discipleship?

These questions help the group apply the truth. As the leader, guide the discussion to move from ideas to action.

Concluding your discussion with personal-application questions is important. Help your group members adopt action steps for applying the truth to their daily lives. Sharing your own personal experiences will help accomplish this task.

Before you conclude in prayer, ask for members' final input or questions. This gives members an opportunity to share or ask things that may not have been considered during the discussion. It creates an environment of openness and shared ownership of the group session by showing that everyone's input is valued.

Session 2: Baptism and the Lord's Supper

Be aware that group members have different experiences or no experience at all with these church practices.

In what ways is baptism an essential part of the Christian life?

In preparation for the group discussion, take time to visit group members who might struggle to understand these concepts.

What's the meaning of baptism?

It's important to help your group members define the terms we use as a church body. These types of content questions will encourage discussion around commonly used terms or phrases. Remember that some in your group may have very little experience in church and are new to these concepts.

Explain why baptism isn't a private act but should be done publicly before the church.

Past experiences are likely to surface in some of the answers given by group members. Bear in mind that experiences help shape our belief systems. Help members root their beliefs in Scripture rather than in experiences.

How does baptism mark you as a member of the church?

This type of question helps the group develop a broader understanding of the Bible. This question requires members to think through various stories of the Book of Acts that weren't discussed. As the leader, be prepared to remind them of stories from the early church or tell them to your group for the first time. Help them integrate a holistic view of the Bible into the conversation.

What does the Lord's Supper cause us to remember?

Based on the biblical texts the group reads, this is a content question that can be quickly answered. Encourage members not just to state the obvious but to dig deeper into the meanings of the verses being discussed.

In the week leading up to the Lord's Supper, how should church members prepare to receive it?

As the leader, make sure you've read all the sessions and viewed all the videos so that you can guide the group.

Should baptism and the Lord's Supper be practiced with a solemn attitude or with a celebrative spirit? Explain your answers.

With some questions you're asking members to reflect on their personal experiences. There's not a right or wrong answer. Rather, you're guiding them to incorporate the truth of the Bible into the regular work of the church. Their emotions will vary in how this occurs.

Before you conclude in prayer, ask for members' final input or questions. This gives members an opportunity to share or ask things that may not have been considered during the discussion. It creates an environment of openness and shared ownership of the group session by showing that everyone's input is valued.

Session 3: Stewardship

Group leaders should always have an awareness of the lives of the group members. Consider how various members will react to dealing with a personal issue like the topic covered in this session.

What difference does it make in your attitude toward tithing and stewardship when you recognize God's ownership of all things?

Asking open-ended questions like this one encourages robust discussion. As you lead the group, try to avoid any questions that can be answered with a simple yes or no. Always invite people to elaborate further on their responses. Your goal is to create discussion so that members assist one another in their discipleship.

What are the things in life with which you have the most trouble being generous?

Asking questions that evoke a testimony, a story, or an emotion is a powerful way to connect group members to one another. This type of question encourages people to share a struggle with a biblical concept. It allows group members to be authentic and receive encouragement.

What do we learn about generosity by understanding that tithing was practiced before God gave the law to the Hebrew people?

Lead group members to understand how all the Bible fits together through these types of questions. You'll encourage them to see how the Old and New Testaments don't contradict but complement each other.

Discuss the impact on your spiritual life when you give from the firstfruits (from the top of what you earn) rather than from what's left over.

Describe the nature of God in giving His Son for our sin.

Questions about the nature and/or role of God help members keep a critical idea at the core of your discussions: God is the main character of the Bible. As you discuss personal experiences and convictions, continue to encourage the group to focus on God's role in the life of the church.

How is stewardship related to the gospel?

The church has many terms that require clear definitions. Take this question as an opportunity to clearly define what your congregation means when it uses the word *gospel*.

How does financial giving aid Christians in their discipleship?

An issue like stewardship can too often be separated from the rest of life. Because money is such an emotional issue, help your group see that it's necessary to consider the implications for the whole life of a disciple.

How can an entire church model stewardship?

What should churches do with the finances they receive?

Follow-up questions are intended to help group members consider how they might be hesitant to truly dig into ideas. These questions move members from ethereal ideas to application.

Before you conclude in prayer, ask for members' final input or questions. This gives members an opportunity to share or ask things that may not have been considered during the discussion. It creates an environment of openness and shared ownership of the group session by showing that everyone's input is valued.

Session 4: Church Discipline

Past experiences often determine our current beliefs. In preparing for this session, consider past experiences in your own life, especially your relationship with your parents. When dealing with the word *discipline,* people will associate it positively or negatively with the authority figures they've had.

When you were a child, what was discipline like?

How does your experience with childhood discipline affect your thoughts about church discipline?

Describe a time in your life when you were the lost sheep or when you witnessed the rescue of a lost sheep.

Personal stories from group members are powerful ways to communicate ways God works through His Word and through the church. Instead of just hoping someone will share a personal story on the spur of the moment, reach out to a member prior to the session and ask him or her to share. Advance notice gives the member an opportunity to gather his or her thoughts for an effective testimony of God's grace.

How does the context of love change the way we initiate church discipline?

What's the ultimate purpose of church discipline?

Questions like this guide the group toward the big ideas that shape our doctrine and practice. We often tend to answer content questions and move on. This question will position church discipline in the larger work of the church's mission.

Notice that Matthew 18:15-20 is preceded by the story of a shepherd who rescues one lost sheep and is followed by the parable of an unforgiving servant. How is your understanding of these verses affected by the surrounding passages?

Context is a key component of a right understanding of the Bible. If the group is large enough, consider having members form smaller groups of two or three persons to discuss this question. Then after a few minutes have each group respond to the larger group.

Why are close relationships necessary for church discipline to accomplish its ultimate task of restoration?

Digging deeper into the practices of the church requires a personal investment of time and relationships. A question like this one assists members to see that church isn't an occurrence but an ongoing covenant relationship with one another.

How can a church create a culture of discipline that's rooted in the gospel?

As you follow up on the idea of creating a culture for ministry, ask members how they see and don't see it happening. As you do, set up healthy boundaries for the discussion in regard to disagreements and complaining.

Groups can discuss vital issues without degenerating into gripe sessions. Rather, as they discuss the truth of the Scriptures, they can do so in a way that encourages one another to engage in healthy disciple making.

Before you conclude in prayer, ask for members' final input or questions. This gives members an opportunity to share or ask things that may not have been considered during the discussion. It creates an environment of openness and shared ownership of the group session by showing that everyone's input is valued.

Session 5: Church Leadership

The goal of the group sessions is to have an open dialogue about biblical issues. If you perceive that members are holding back from the discussion, talk to them individually to discover the reasons. Help them understand that they play vital roles in the life of the group.

This session's discussion comes in the context of the way your church chooses, installs, and supports its leaders. You may discover that your church has a slightly or altogether different model for leadership than what's described in this study. If that's the case, discuss it with your church leaders prior to the group session. As members of the group point this out, take the opportunity to alert them that you've discussed these differences with the leaders. Or invite one of the leaders to attend the group discussion.

Describe the difference between the two roles of elder and deacon.

Using questions that contrast two ideas helps members understand nuances of biblical teaching. Even though the answer is obvious, some people have less experience studying the Bible. Lead the discussion in such a way that it's easy for everyone to participate.

What are some major characteristics we should look for in potential elders?

Consider using a sheet of poster board for questions that require lists for the answers. Some group members are better at answering questions when they have a visual representation of the answer.

What type of attitude should elders have toward a congregation?

When we ask about attitudes of leaders, it may bring up a number of past experiences, both positive and negative. In discussing what should be, some members may want to discuss what's occurred in the past. As the leader, determine ahead of time what direction you want this discussion to take.

What are some major characteristics we should look for in potential deacons?

What does the word *likewise* in I Timothy 3:8 signal to us?

Discussing particular words and phrases of a biblical text requires some extra work. To address a question like this one, encourage a group member ahead of time to study the issue and be prepared to give an answer. By doing so, you'll give the group a head start on the discussion. You'll also encourage personal Bible study.

What were the responsibilities of the first men who served in deaconlike ministry?

Because of their faithfulness what was the result in the church?

Answering a question like this one about the biblical text naturally leads into a discussion about its current implications. You can easily use a follow-up question of your own, such as "In what ways does the work of deacons today aid the rest of our church?"

How do the roles of elders and deacons aid in keeping God's Word as a priority in the church?

Describe the way members of the congregation should relate to and feel about their leaders.

Asking for an emotional response from the group members will be comfortable for some members but not all. Emotions are a normal part of life and aren't avoided by the Bible. Some members are more emotionally oriented than others, but help all members understand that God desires us to relate positively to one another.

Before you conclude in prayer, ask for members' final input or questions. This gives members an opportunity to share or ask things that may not have been considered during the discussion. It creates an environment of openness and shared ownership of the group session by showing that everyone's input is valued.

Session 6: The Great Commission

Every organization has a reason for its existence. You may want to open the session by reading various mission statements of well-known companies, charities, or organizations to prepare members for the final discussion.

> **How does the promise of Jesus' presence with the disciples change the way we go about fulfilling the Great Commission?**

Questions about God's role in the mission of the church help members understand God's priorities. A question like this one requires members to expand on an idea. Encourage them to use biblical, historical, and current examples of ways God's presence makes a difference in the church's mission.

> **When you feel fearful, nervous, or anxious about sharing the gospel with another person, how will Matthew 28:16-20 change your attitude?**

When you ask for members to share doubts and fears, they'll likely identify specific fears they face. Carefully listen to their answers and don't let any members denigrate others' emotions.

> **What part of the Great Commission is your church doing very well? What part needs more attention?**

Keep a positive attitude in discussing both the strengths and challenges of your local church. Don't allow personal insults to persist in the discussion. Instead, ask members to take personal ownership of struggles by the church. Also lead them to praise God for ways He's working through the church.

> **What's the difference between the way a convert lives and the way a disciple lives?**

How would you like to refine the scorecard in the church to better reflect Jesus' priorities in the Great Commission?

These two questions ask the group to respond the video teaching. Pastor Robby's term *scorecard* in the video may be unusual for some members, even off-putting. Help them understand the spirit of his comments so that they can discuss how we discern the positive movement of church ministry.

Describe from 2 Timothy 2:2 the way Timothy was to pass along the truth of God's Word.

What does Paul's instruction to Timothy teach us about carrying out the Great Commission?

Ask for various ways to answer this question. You may consider looking for verbal, visual, or even mathematical equations that represent 2 Timothy 2:2. Encourage the group to be creative in the way they answer questions.

By relating Paul's message to Jesus' Great Commission, you can help the group connect the dots throughout all the Bible. Encourage members to identify other passages that inform our understanding of God's commission to the church.

Consider the idea that Jesus was overjoyed by the work of the disciples. What work of your local church gives Jesus joy?

End the study with a positive note of God's love for His church. A positive note doesn't exclude conviction but points toward God's ultimate purpose for His people.

Tips for Leading a Small Group

Prayerfully Prepare

Prepare for each group session with prayer. Ask the Holy Spirit to work through you and the group discussion as you point to Jesus each week through God's Word.

REVIEW the weekly material and group questions ahead of time.

PRAY for each person in the group.

Minimize Distractions

Do everything in your ability to help people focus on what's most important: connecting with God, with the Bible, and with one another. Create a comfortable environment. If group members are uncomfortable, they'll be distracted and therefore not engaged in the group experience. Take into consideration seating, temperature, lighting, refreshments, surrounding noise, and general cleanliness.

At best, thoughtfulness and hospitality show guests and group members they're welcome and valued in whatever environment you choose to gather. At worst, people may never notice your effort, but they're also not distracted.

Include Others

Your goal is to foster a community in which people are welcome just as they are but encouraged to grow spiritually. Always be aware of opportunities to include and invite.

INVITE new people to join your group.

INCLUDE anyone who visits the group.

Encourage Discussion

A good small-group experience has the following characteristics.

EVERYONE PARTICIPATES. Encourage everyone to ask questions, share responses, or read aloud.

NO ONE DOMINATES—NOT EVEN THE LEADER. Be sure your time speaking as a leader takes up less than half your time together as a group. Politely guide discussion if anyone dominates.

NOBODY IS RUSHED THROUGH QUESTIONS. Don't feel that a moment of silence is a bad thing. People often need time to think about their responses to questions they've just heard or to gain courage to share what God is stirring in their hearts.

INPUT IS AFFIRMED AND FOLLOWED UP. Make sure you point out something true or helpful in a response. Don't just move on. Build community with follow-up questions, asking how other people have experienced similar things or how a truth has shaped their understanding of God and the Scripture you're studying. People are less likely to speak up if they fear that you don't actually want to hear their answers or that you're looking for only a certain answer.

GOD AND HIS WORD ARE CENTRAL. Opinions and experiences can be helpful, but God has given us the truth. Trust Scripture to be the authority and God's Spirit to work in people's lives. You can't change anyone, but God can. Continually point people to the Word and to active steps of faith.

KEEP CONNECTING

Think of ways to connect with group members during the week. Participation during the group session is always improved when members spend time connecting with one another outside the group sessions. The more people are comfortable with and involved in one another's lives, the more they'll look forward to being together. When people move beyond being friendly to truly being friends who form a community, they come to each session eager to engage instead of merely attending.

Encourage group members with thoughts, commitments, or questions from the session by connecting through emails, texts, and social media.

Build deeper friendships by planning or spontaneously inviting group members to join you outside your regularly scheduled group time for meals; fun activities; and projects around your home, church, or community.

Group Information

NAME   **CONTACT**